EDUCATION
OR DOMINATION?

*A Critical Look at Educational
Problems Today*

Edited by Douglas Holly

Arrow Books

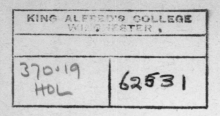
Arrow Books Limited
3 Fitzroy Square, London W1

London Melbourne Sydney Auckland
Wellington Johannesburg Cape Town
and agencies throughout the world

First published in Arrow Books Ltd 1974
Introduction and The Invisible Ruling Class
© Douglas Holly 1974
Education and Politics © Ted Benton 1974
Economists and 'Human Capital' © Adam Westoby 1974
Language and Class © Harold Rosen 1972
The Politics of Culture © Graham Murdock 1974
Integrating Art into Society © Ian Jeffrey 1974
Education, Race and Society © Charles Husband 1974
The School and the Community © Ken Warpole 1974
Relationships Among Teachers © Arnold Downes 1974
The Free Schoolers © Guy Neave 1974

Set in Monotype Times
Printed in Great Britain by The Anchor Press Ltd
and bound by Wm Brendon & Son Ltd
both of Tiptree, Essex

ISBN 0 09 909580 7

Contents

Introduction

Douglas Holly

This collection of writings on education is aimed not so much at the 'experts' in education – though it has a great deal to say to them too – as at the sort of men and women who are concerned about the way our schools are today and who are trying to understand the causes of problems which they see their own children experiencing. Some of these problems are hardly new – overcrowding, inadequate facilities for learning, stupid administrative practices, the parish-pump mentality of some head teachers and local authorities. But other problems are new – or are taking on a new significance. These include the continuing struggle between reformers and conservatives over comprehensive reorganization and updated curriculum, the claims that the language of ordinary people somehow holds back the educational progress of their children, the growing refusal of pupils themselves to submit to repressive attitudes on the part of teachers and head teachers, the question of immigrant pupils, and the emergence of a new spirit among some teachers, especially younger ones who are calling for greater democracy, closer links between schools and the outside world and – in extreme cases – for a break-away from ordinary schools altogether.

What are people to make of all this? What is really new in the situation and what is actually a crystallization of things that have been there all the time? How do the problems of children in schools link up with the problems that are familiar to people in their working lives? These and other questions are what interest the writers in this book. It is usually difficult for the lay reader to penetrate the verbiage of educational writing, largely because educational writing is often a determined attempt to pretend that education is some sort of privileged area of life separate from the large issues which fill the newspapers and television screens and separate also from the ordinary day-to-day concerns of trade unionist and housewife. This book is dedicated to dispelling these mists and making the connections – social, political and cultural – apparent. We live in a society dominated skilfully by faceless people who would like us all to remain under the impression that we are puny, powerless, mere cogs in the social and industrial machine. Although they may differ from one another on many points, the contributors to this collection are united in one belief at least – the belief that ordinary working people can and must learn to understand the basic mechanisms of our society, of which education is a key area. If politics is too important to be left to the politicians, education is certainly too important to be left to the educationalists.

March 1974   **Douglas Holly**

1. Education and Politics

Ted Benton

Introduction

One of the favourite ideas of those who want to keep things in Britain more or less unchanged in their basic essentials is that education is an area of life quite separate from all others. Because it has to do with children it should be kept pure and unsullied by adult affairs – like politics – for instance. It is supposed to be indecent to mention political and educational ideas in the same breath. Such an idea does no justice to the true nature of education, and little justice to the real meaning of politics. Ted Benton seeks to show that education and politics are in fact closely connected aspects of our lives in society. The issue in Britain today is much more complex in some ways but far simpler in others than any of the main political groups appear to realize.

Ted Benton was educated at City of Leicester College of Education. He taught physics and biology in a Leicestershire Plan Junior High School for a time, and then went to take degrees in philosophy at Leicester and Oxford Universities. He now teaches in the Sociology Department of Essex University.

First it may be necessary to deal with a certain squeamishness which most of us experience when the terms 'politics' and 'education' are conjoined. In the public debate about education, distinctions are often drawn between educationally and politically motivated reforms (or opposition to reform); between educational aims, and political aims in education. It was commonplace, for instance, for Conservative opponents of Labour's comprehensivization programme to stigmatize it as politically motivated. Equally, many on the political left have chastised Conservative opposition to comprehensivization and the Tory slow-down of reorganization as doctrinaire and politically motivated, claiming that a comprehensive secondary system is necessary for purely educational reasons. Yet, when the 'purely educational' arguments on both sides are specified – preservation of choice, unity of the educational process, failings of early selection, maintaining academic standards, catering for the able child, catering for aptitude as well as ability, wider access to scarce equipment and other resources and so on – it is possible to show that each one belongs to a broader framework of ideas or ideology which, in turn, expresses a definite political commitment.

Indeed, the very distinction educational/political in this sort of context is itself ideological. The notion at work is that education like the rest of the institutions of the state (what I shall refer to as 'state apparatuses') is neutral with respect to the struggles and conflicts going on elsewhere in society. The state as a whole is a neutral arbiter, an honest broker, which stands above the multiplicity of competing interests and pressures at work in civil society. If the state as a whole must remain neutral, then even more must this be so for the complex of educational institutions to whose care is entrusted the tender, impressionable mind of the new generation. Education must be kept out of politics and politics out of education!

The full answer to this point of view actually involves alternative concepts of politics and education. But even if we take for granted at this stage the commonly accepted notion of politics as a means by which scarce resources ('goods' of various sorts) are distributed throughout the population, and by which this distribution is legitimated, then it is plain that all major decisions which affect the access of the population to educational resources are *political* decisions. This is, of course, just as much so if the decision in question is *not* to make any changes, as if the decision is to instigate a major reform. To argue that a decision which will inevitably be political in its effects must, nevertheless, be made from motives, or with aims in mind, which are purely educational, is merely to ask for a political action to be presented in a non-political disguise: it is a demand for mystification.

Educational practice, then, and the decisions which affect it, belong to the field of political debate and political struggle; they cannot logically be taken out of it. Instead of pretending that this is not so, we should declare our interests and take sides. But a condition of effectively taking sides is that we understand the forms and conditions of our struggle. In the present case this understanding involves the labour of acquiring and producing theoretical knowledge, not just of the educational system, but also of the whole social system to which it belongs. Because of this, I must begin by dealing with questions which at first seem a long way from the question of education.

As the terms 'politics' and 'state' will appear frequently in what follows, I had better begin by saying roughly what I shall mean by them. First, the state. In *The Origin of the Family, Private Property and the State*, Engels uses the term state to refer centrally to 'special bodies of armed men' (army, police), arising out of society and placing themselves above it. Adjuncts of these special bodies of armed men are the prisons and courts of law, together with a body of officials with the power to levy taxes. A state in this sense only arises in a society where irreconcilably antagonistic classes threaten to 'consume themselves and society in sterile struggle'. The state serves to moderate the conflict between classes, to keep it within certain bounds; to maintain a degree of order. Where other notions of the state have it arbitrating between competing interests – i.e. effecting a reconciliation between them – for Engels, the very existence of the state, for all its moderating of class conflict, is a mark of the irreconcilability of that conflict. The state, far from being neutral with respect to competing interests in society, is a machine by which a dominant class maintains its domination. For the politically dominant class, usually also the economically dominant class, the state is principally a means of 'holding down and exploiting the oppressed class'.

This Marxist view is broadly the conception of the state which I shall adopt in this paper, and in defence of which I shall present arguments as we continue. However, one rather important modification is required. It is this: in speaking of the armed forces, the police, the courts and the central administration, Engels deals with that part of the state which functions mainly by physical force or administrative coercion. In other words, he identifies the state with what have elsewhere been called 'the repressive state apparatuses'. Recent direct use of police against pickets, the trial for conspiracy of building workers' pickets and the jailing of five dockers illustrate this feature of the functioning of the state in Britain. Other, perhaps more dramatic, examples could be given from other countries. But what Engels does not deal with as part of the state is that institutional complex which does not function predominantly by repression, but which nevertheless has strong claims to be included within the state. Here may be included the communications media, the educational system, the churches, the political system, the trade unions, and, perhaps, the family. Now, whether or not all these institutions belong to the state in the juridical sense, it can be argued that their functioning within the social system resembles that of the other apparatuses of the state. That is to say, they operate to hold down and sustain the exploitation of one or more oppressed classes by a dominant class. However, they differ from the other state apparatuses in that they function predominantly by ideology, rather than by violence or the threat of it. For this reason, the French Marxist, Louis Althusser, has extended the reference of the term 'state' to include these ideological state apparatuses.

Since the educational system figures as one of the most important of these apparatuses in capitalist societies, it is perhaps worth saying a little more about *how* they function to sustain exploitation. First, what are the basic requirements for the continuity of economic production in any form of society? It is clear that, since raw materials and human energy get used up, and instruments of production and human beings wear out, production can only be sustained if these various factors of production are constantly being replaced. Also, the replacements must be of the right type, in the right quantities and proportions, and in the right relationships.

As continuous production is a condition of the survival of every society, it follows that every society must make provision for this constant renewal of the conditions of production. Further, in all *class* societies (i.e. societies in which a class of direct *producers* of wealth is continuously exploited by a class of non-producing *owners* of wealth), those institutions whose function is to reproduce the conditions of production, in so doing reproduce, or sustain, the relationship of economic exploitation between the social classes. This amounts to saying that such institutions play a part in reproducing the social classes themselves.

This, I shall be arguing, is the main (though not the sole) function of the educational system in capitalist societies. So, for example, when the various mechanisms of selection which operate in the educational system segregate and distribute children according to their estimated ability or potential (i.e. their predicted place in the class structure) in order that they can undergo different processes of training and preparation, this is not some politically neutral exercise whose sole concern is the development of the child. The necessary attitudes, skills and disciplines are being inculcated into the appropriate individuals in the appropriate proportions for the requirements of the capitalist–labour market.

That, of course, is an enormous over-simplification. The educational system is not a well-oiled, frictionless machine, neatly interlocked with the labour market. Nor does it operate upon an inert and malleable raw material! Kids resist being educated to a greater or lesser extent, and in many different ways. One of the things that makes this possible is the variety of agencies other than the school which play a part in forming them as social beings.

If we consider the working class child, these will include his family, the broader social relationships of his parents, the traditional practices, games and rituals of his neighbourhood gangs, which may in turn bring him into direct relation to the police (his first direct experience of the repressive state apparatus!) and the authority they impose on him. This may be very important (note, for instance, the ubiquitous presence of both police and teachers in comics with a mainly working class readership, and the complex and subtle structure that is depicted in them). Even the geography of his area, the social relations reflected in the street design, the residential separation of the classes, the differential presence of the redevelopers, play a part in forming him ideologically, that is to say, in producing the more or less contradictory unity of thought and practice that will be distinctively his.

In so far as many working class children share these determinants of their behaviour and attitudes and in so far as, in these respects, they will differ from children from other social classes, we should expect quite different ways of relating to and understanding the experience of school. And in so far as these different orientations to school which are characteristic of the different social classes give rise to forms of *resistance* to schooling (truancy, day-dreaming, playing-up teacher, the use of physical violence against teachers and school property) it is possible to speak of class struggle in the schools. This is so *whether or not* those who resist are conscious of the class nature of their resistance.

A rather obvious example of the way in which friction arises between the educational and economic systems is the way in which the technical division of labour in industry requires that a certain proportion of those entering the labour market at any one time have a particular level and sort of scientific knowledge. If the educational system is to meet this requirement then the demand must find its way back to a certain redistribution of pupils into science specializations in the more academic sector. If the educational system is to continue to operate predominantly by ideology rather than repression, this distribution of students must be experienced by them as a choice. When passive student resistance to this sort of distribution emerges either some new coercive techniques have to be introduced (higher admission standards for arts subjects, etc.) or the educational system simply fails to meet the requirements of the labour market.

With the above as a broad theoretical framework, I can now turn to the job of analysing and criticizing the conceptions of education involved in the education policies of a number of organizations on the left. I'll begin with a discussion of some central ideological currents in the educational thinking of the Labour party.

One strand within the broadly egalitarian ideology of the party since its origins has been the objective of 'equality of opportunity'. As Michael Parkinson points out, 'The Labour Party . . . has been anxious that the principle of equality of opportunity for all individuals and social groups should operate in this area of social arrangements which so directly affects the distribution of social and economic rewards.' From the beginning the party supported educational reform which showed promise of extending educational opportunity for working class children. It supported the 1918 Fisher Education Act for this reason, despite some reservations about the limited *extent* of the progress it represented. The party's own policy statement of 1918, *Labour and the New Social Order*, was critical of the existing educational system in that it 'still reserved the endowed secondary schools, and even more the universities, for the most part, to the sons and daughters of a small privileged class . . .'. The enormously influential book by R. H. Tawney, *Secondary Education for All*, which appeared in 1922, was predominantly devoted to putting forward the implications of another ideal of equality ('equality of provision') but it repeatedly connected the call for increased provision of education with the existing absence of *opportunity* in education for working class children. In fact, the main achievements in the educational field of the two inter-war Labour governments were both related to increasing educational opportunities for working class children: there was a general increase in the proportion of free places in secondary schools offered by the L E As from 25 per cent to 50 per cent, and an earlier limit on maintencance allowances for needy children was removed.

In terms of this perspective either education itself, or,

more often, the social rewards which it brings to the educated (i.e. 'qualified') individual, are regarded as goods in relatively scarce supply. Given that any foreseeable increase in supply of these goods would not allow their equal distribution, the central problem becomes how to secure social justice in their unequal distribution. The solution, of course, is competition on equal terms – a race in which everyone at least *starts* at the same point. The equality of opportunity perspective then poses as the central axis around which to organize knowledge of education and programmes for its reform, the question of handicaps and advantages in the race for educational success.

A dominant though never universal and now quite defensive tradition in the sociology of education adopts this conceptual framework, as can be checked by a fairly brief examination of any standard textbook. The sections on social mobility through education, the effects of economic situations, values, early socialization and linguistic practices, on educational achievement, the nature of educational selection mechanisms, and so on, are replete with statistical and bibliographical material. In the more critical texts, which include chapters on education and the state, on education and social change and on other fields less readily related to the equality of opportunity perspective, one may find plenty in the way of promises for the future, but very little in the way of hard research to report.

The political implications of the equality of opportunity perspective are fairly clear. Once it is established that working class children are disadvantaged in the educational system, attempts must be made to intervene in the processes which give rise to these disadvantages. Abolition of fee-paying, provision of maintenance allowances, attempts to alter cultural characteristics and/or values of working class children or parents, alteration of formal selection mechanisms used by the schools and other proposals are all directed at improving the educational and hence occupational opportunities of working class children.

So what is wrong with this perspective? First, it is capable of posing, at most, the possibility of altering the chances of a small minority of individuals, since it takes for granted the existing educational and occupational hierarchies and poses *access* to them as the central problem. The aspirations of the *mass* of working class people for a better life (as opposed to the *chance* of one for some of their children) could only be met by a fundamental change of political, economic and social relationships, that is to say, by a challenge to the existing system of class domination. Such a challenge cannot be provided by this ideology or by a political practice based on it, since to adopt the problem of recruitment into the social classes as the central problem is to relegate to the periphery the problem of the relationships between the classes themselves. A related point is that this perspective is defective in presenting the educational system as if its sole function were to be analysed exhaustively in terms of its selection mechanisms and their effects. What is usually called the socializing function of the schools – what I have called their part in the reproduction of the social classes – is largely ignored within this perspective except in so far as the content, styles of communication and social relationships of the teaching process have themselves something to do with selection mechanisms.

The dominance of the equality of opportunity perspective in the sociology of education is paralleled by a similar dominance of economics and political science by theories which organize their respective fields in terms of the categories of competition for scarce resources. The historical origins of this structure of thought as a major social force are to be found in the seventeenth and eighteenth century social and political philosophies of the rising European bourgeoisie. Indeed the bourgeois character of this perspective is so very obvious that what requires explanation is the credibility it has had with the left in this country. A large part of this credibility, it seems, dreived from the fact that in its most influential formulations the doctrine of equality of opportunity has appeared combined with other concepts.

Tawney and more recent Labour intellectuals such as A. H. Halsely and Basil Bernstein – through successive revisions and disclaimers – combine the perspective of equality of opportunity with the concept of social class. It is not just that certain *individuals* are disadvantaged in the race, but there is a pattern to the disadvantages: they are related to the social class of the disadvantaged. To speak of social classes, and of their inequality, is frequently taken as the hallmark of the radical – hence the credibility of this sort of doctrine on the left. However, independently of the motives or genuine sympathies of those concerned, this credence is misplaced. As Marx himself pointed out, the existence of classes was no discovery of his; it had a distinguished history in bourgeois thought. Moreover, the particular conception of class which is combined with the notion of equality of opportunity in education is a rather impoverished one (more about this later), and it plays an entirely secondary role in relation to its partner.

Another important strand in the Labour party's educational ideology is now to be found fused with the first. The combination first appeared as a major social force in Labour's electoral strategy prior to the 1964 election. After nearly two decades without mass unemployment, large sections of organized labour had more than kept pace in terms of income with the lower ranks of white-collar workers. Some of the physical stress had been removed from some manual jobs, and technological development seemed to some to show the prospect of abolishing some of the most debilitating of manual occupations altogether. Consumer durables had become more widely available, at least to those sections of the working class which had benefited from strong trade union organization in expanding, usually technically advanced, industries. But despite the undoubted advance in living standards for some sections of the working class, there was little alteration of income differentials if the whole occupational spectrum was considered, while economic wealth and power continued to be concentrated into a very few hands.

Nevertheless, the very real changes which had certainly taken place supported a widespread *belief* that economic inequalities were being reduced. Even where this belief was not accepted the recognition of absolute improvements, despite continuing inequality, made economic equality seem a much less important objective. In general, the changes which were noted in the social and political debate of the time seemed strikingly to share a common feature: *technological innovation was heavily involved*. This gave added plausibility and immediate topicality to what was really quite an old-established conception of society and social change. According to this conception the general characteristics of any society – its political institutions, its ideas and general culture, the character of its social relationships – are all determined by its level of *technical development*. Also, technical development is the main cause of all forms of social and cultural developments, so that, in general, the progress of mankind comes to be seen as assured, given that all irrational obstacles to technological development are removed. This ideology of progress, technological determinism, is often mistakenly attributed to Marx, even though it was widespread in his day and Marx was a great opponent of it.

In the early and middle sixties variants of this ideology proliferated on an enormous scale. The logic of industrialism, convergence, the end of ideology, mass society, became fashionable notions, and all shared the common denominator of technological determination of progress. On the left, too, thinkers like Marcuse attributed enormous causal importance to technology. Meanwhile, in this broad economic, social and intellectual setting further changes were taking place within the Labour party itself. The long-term significance of these changes seems to have been a shift in decision-making power within the party in favour of managerial professional workers against unskilled and semi-skilled manual workers, while sociological studies of the period indicate a distinctive orientation towards the party on the part of rank and file voters in the more affluent sections of the working class – an orientation described by one study as 'instrumental' (see Goldthorpe, Lockwood et al., 1968, and Hindess, 1971).

The ideology which gained dominance within the party at this time, and which must have played some considerable part in winning over a large proportion of lower white-collar workers to the party, was, not surprisingly, a form of technological determinism. The next Labour government would devote itself to the only task left open to political intervention by the determinist ideology – that of sweeping away irrational and anachronistic obstacles to the white heat of the technological revolution.

Of course, one of the main obstacles to social progress conceived in these terms was the old school tie. For instance, in *Signposts for the Sixties* (Labour Party, eighth reprint, June 1963, p. 10) we read:

With certain honourable exceptions, our finance and industry need a major shake-up at the top. Too many directors owe their position to family, school or political connections. If the dead wood were cut out of Britain's board-rooms and replaced by the keen young executives, production engineers and scientists who are at present denied their legitimate prospects of promotion, our production and export problems would be much more manageable.

Wilson took enormous pride in pointing out in 1964 that no one in his government had been to any of *his* old schools – though over 40 per cent of his 1967 cabinet had been to public schools (Rubinstein and Stoneman, 1972, p. 85).

Technological progress had, it was argued, transformed the manpower requirements of the economy. An increasing proportion of highly skilled and technically educated men was required. For the educational system one clear implication was drawn: there must be an overall increase in the provision of education – and particularly science education – that is, an increase in investment in 'human capital'. Even more important, measures had to be taken to reduce the *wastage* of valuable human capital: the rate of drop-out from education of talented children with working class origins had to be stemmed. Equality of opportunity, involving both equal access to educational qualification, and access to occupations based on the level of achieved qualifications, was now presented as a demand imposed on the education system by economic and technical necessity. Again in *Signposts for the Sixties* (p. 28), we read: 'Children are the nation's most valuable asset. What we spend on their schooling earns a bigger return in the quality of our national life than any other expenditure. This is more true than ever in the age of scientific revolution, when the improvement of our living standards and our survival as a free democracy depend largely upon the quality of our scientific, technological and technical education.' There was thus a convenient coincidence of aims between the sort of dilute egalitarianism discussed earlier, and the newly dominant technological determinist ideology.

In so far as the policy implications of this new ideology were identical with those of the equality of opportunity perspective, they require no further criticism. But, in fact, the broader ideology did have broader implications. Since technology was perceived as the main agent of social progress, a *general* subordination of the educational system to the requirements of economic development was called for. This allowed debate to broaden from a narrow concern with selection mechanisms and social mobility to a consideration of the nature and content of the learning process, and the structure of relationships in which it took place. In particular, it was now possible to devote attention to the nature of education not just as an avenue of social mobility for a few, but as *preparation* for adult life and adult *occupational* life in particular. The distribution of resources to the different sectors within education should be explicitly governed by the levels and proportions of the different skills, competences and knowledges required and expected to be required by the economy. The kind of training given in the schools and colleges should reflect in content and method the future occupations of the students.

It would be difficult to overestimate the tremendous power and diffusion of this form of the technological ideology; it pervaded almost the whole spectrum of progressive writing on education in the mid-sixties, and its dominance is still hardly diminished. For example, in *The Red Paper* (eds, R. Cuddihy, D. Cowan, C. Lindsay, p. 3) we read:

The responsibility of people playing leading roles in education is . . . to help teachers move forward to educational practices which are appropriate to our fast-changing, ever-demanding, technological society.

Also, in the same collection, Eric Robinson says:

Technical teachers who would strenuously deny any taint of liberalism are teaching to your unacademic apprentices principles of mathematics and science that twenty years ago were regarded as sophisticated academic work. *They cannot help themselves because technical progress demands it.* (p. 15, my italics)

What then are the main points of criticism to be levelled against this technological ideology? They are, I think, the following:

(a) In this type of thinking, *technological* development is never clearly distinguished from *economic* development. The term technology refers primarily to the means by which commodities are produced, and sometimes to the commodities so produced. But any adequate conception of the economy must take into account the whole structure of social relationships in which production and the distribution of the product takes place. These will include relations of power and authority, powerlessness and subordination, and, above all, relations of property.

The political effects of this particular confusion are important. In particular the question of *which class interests* are served by an educational system subordinated to a capitalist economic system simply cannot be raised within such a perspective. Thus, for instance, Banks in her book *Sociology of Education* feels able to compare countries as diverse as the USA, USSR and Britain with respect to the effect of the economy on the scope and content of education without taking into account differences in their systems of property ownership.

(b) Though the ideology recognizes that education selects and prepares individuals for the occupational structure, it fundamentally misconceives the occupational structure. The central misconception is to suppose that the occupational structure of a society at any moment is a direct effect of the division of labour imposed by the given level of technological development. Firstly, not all occupations are located in the economic structure, and many of those that are not (including politics, the armed forces, medicine, education itself) retain a certain degree of autonomy from the economy. This alone is sufficient to show the fallacy of relying upon technical development to yield general social and cultural advancement. Secondly, an occupational role even *in* the economic structure is not simply a position in the technical division of labour – i.e. it consists of more than the exercise of certain technical skills and knowledge. A person who performs an occupational role stands in a whole complex of power and authority relations, and his performance in that role will be subject to expectations, obligations and standards of various, sometimes mutually contradictory, sorts. The confusion between the occupational role and what we might term the technical role is the counterpart of the confusion between economy and technology. It, too, has fairly obvious political effects. In the grip of this ideological conflation it is impossible to distinguish those aspects of learning which constitute the acquisition of new socially necessary skills and techniques from those which constitute the crucial ideological training for the place the student is to occupy in the structure of power and authority relations which is woven into the occupational structure.

The desirability of giving more children the chance to acquire technical skills and knowledge, which are in ever-increasing demand as society advances, seems hardly questionable as a social goal. But if the – perhaps unintended – consequence of pursuit of those goals were understood to be the further subordination of the educational system to this ideological moulding of individuals for the requirements of the capitalist organization of production and social relationships generally, then perhaps it would be a little more politically contentious within the ranks of the Labour party.

Thirdly – and this comes out very clearly in the type of

sociological work referred to above – the occupational
structure is seen primarily as a hierarchy of rewards either
of status or income. But positions in the occupational
structure are related to one another in a whole variety of
ways, of which higher and lower, more and less are merely
a small sample. In capitalist societies, for instance, the
production worker does not simply have a lower income
than, say, the university professor. He also *produces* the
wealth which provides the professor's greater income, whilst
the professor himself produces no wealth at all. Similarly,
the major shareholder not only has a greater income than
the worker he employs but he also *disposes over* the means
of production, access to which is the condition of existence
of the worker and his family. The neglect of these features
of the occupational structure yields an impoverished concept of social class, in terms of which the lower range of
occupations constitute the working – or lower – class, the
middle range of the middle class, and so on. This is to be
contrasted with the much more fruitful Marxist concept of
class in which the relations of production are the basis for
the formation of classes as mutually antagonistic social
forces engaged in struggles of different forms and inten-
sities at the different economic, political and ideological
levels of society. (See Poulantzas, 1973.)

Impoverished conceptions of occupational structure and
class, of course, have their political effects. If one class, or
one section of it, is deprived or underprivileged with
respect to others this simply means it has less of something
– self-esteem, income, say in decisions, linguistic competences, etc. The policy implication is clear: give it more,
redistribute!

Such a conception of class in fact prevents the adequate
posing of the question to what extent inequalities in the
distribution of these goods is a function of the system of
class domination (class here being used in the fuller sense

outlined above). The general failure of systematic attempts at income redistribution, as well as attempts at redistributing the rather less readily measurable goods that go to make up educational opportunity – i.e. the failure to date of programmes of compensatory education of all kinds – is one indication that such inequalities are, indeed, to a very *great* extent functions of the system of class domination. If this is so, then the political implication would seem to be that only a shift in the relation of forces between the classes in struggle could achieve even the limited objectives of the equality of opportunity brigade.

(c) The third line of criticism of Labour's technological ideology of education is this: the educational system, in conducting the necessary ideological and technical preparation of children for adult roles, is not simply preparing them for *occupational* roles, as presupposed in this ideology of education. Although most pupils are not destined to be full-time trade union officials, M Ps, party agents or clergymen they do receive at school the rudiments of political and religious ideologies. These prepare them for limited participation as adults in the institutions and rituals in which these ideologies are materialized such as the church, the political parties, elections, marriages, funerals, etc. Even more importantly, the educational system plays a large role in inculcating the relevant skills and subjection to the relevant ideological dispositions of women in preparation for their role in the division of labour within the capitalist family. Equally the almost complete absence of training in these skills – domestic science, hygiene, etc. – for boys tends to reinforce a complementary ideology in them. As to the detailed mechanisms by which these ideologies are inculcated and the effects on them of, for instance, sexual segregation versus coeducation, little is known as yet, but investigations provoked by, or carried out within, the movement for women's liberation are at least ensuring that these questions are being posed.

There are, of course, ideological currents within Labour's educational thinking other than the two which I have characterized as equality of opportunity and technological determinism, and there are more ways of combining them than in the one example I have selected. I can give some indication of the complexity involved in the problem by briefly examining the debate about secondary reorganization within the Labour movement. Dennis Marsden (*Politicians, Equality and the Comprehensiveness*) provides a useful preliminary distinction between three sorts of goals for comprehensive education. The meritocratic view corresponds rather closely to the ideology which I labelled equality of opportunity. On this view, the advantage of comprehensivization over the existing tripartite system is that the possibility of educational success remains open throughout the educational career of each child. The mechanisms of selection at work are much more efficient in avoiding wastage of talent, and ensuring the fullest development of the talent which is selected. A varient of this perspective, not mentioned by Marsden, combines it with the technological determinist ideology – the reorganization of the secondary system so as to avoid wastage of talent is dictated by the changing manpower requirements of advanced industrial societies. Further, the common core of *general* education which can best be provided within a unitary system has also been argued as the most appropriate form of educational preparation for flexible labour force in a rapidly changing economy, i.e. one in which *technical* change is rapid.

Secondly, Marsden distinguishes what he calls the social engineering approach. The idea here is that the advantages of the comprehensive school in providing greater oppor-

tunities in education can be combined with advantages
derived from opportunities for greater social mixing in the
school. On this pattern, the comprehensives would remain
streamed and would not introduce major curricular reforms, though around the curriculum would be built
provision for social mixing between the different classes
and ability levels. This Crosland version (C. A. R. Crosland, *The Future of Socialism,* esp. Ch. XII) of the comprehensive schools sees it as a means of doing away with
resentment, envy and all the attributes of old-fashioned
class division. Given the assumption that the economic inequalities between classes are becoming less and less significant, the class system is seen now as an anachronistic
system of inequalities of status and prestige, sustained to a
large degree by such institutions as the tripartite division in
education – yielding, on the one hand, snobbishness and a
feeling of superiority, on the other hand resentment and a
feeling of failure. Here again we have a vision of technological changes leading the way to progress, the role
of politics being merely to clear away obsolete obstacles –
such as class consciousness – from the path of this progress.

The shortcoming of this argument, of course, is that since
its basic premise – the ending of any real basis for class
differences – isn't true (see, for instance, Blackburn's
article in *Towards Socialism* and Westergaard's in *Ideology
in Social Science*) then class consciousness is not anachronistic at all. A reorganization of the educational
system which succeeded in educating working class
children *out* of thinking of society in terms of class division,
whilst society remained deeply class divided, would represent a serious setback for the whole workers' movement.
Fortunately, what little evidence is available seems to
indicate that the comprehensive school by no means has
the sort of ideological effects that Crosland and others had
anticipated (see J. Ford, 1969).

There exists as yet, however, very little evidence on what precisely the effects of reorganization *are* on the capacity of the educational system to allocate and prepare children ideologically for their future roles in the division of labour. Both the tripartite systems and the elementary/secondary system which preceded it, in all their local variations, involved the segregated reproduction of the working class, of the intermediate clerical, technical and professional workers, and – through the system of private schools – of the ruling class and its leading agencies in the judiciary, politics, civil service and armed forces (see Rosenberg, p. 7). Though in each case it is overwhelmingly the ideology of the ruling class which is inculcated, it is inculcated in different forms and through different mechanisms according to the social destination of its recipients. Separate school systems, with different structures of authority, different curricula, different daily rituals and so on provide the sort of context in which this social differentiation can readily be effected. But the difficulties of achieving this task within the confines of a unitary institutional structure are quite obvious. A good deal of conservative opposition to comprehensives is quite explicitly motivated by fear. How are the special qualities of leadership to be selected and nurtured within the context of a school designed to provide the masses of the led with the necessary rudiments of culture? Hopefully, these conservative fears may be well founded. Reorganization does present serious obstacles to the hegemony of the dominant ideology within the educational system. In other words the comprehensive school may well turn out to provide a better environment for teachers and pupils opposed to that hegemony to carry on their struggle.

But the social engineering justification for comprehensive reorganization is interesting in another respect: it involves a commitment to the idea of using educational reforms as a means of producing social equality – conceived in terms of status and social mixing. This feature is shared with the third of Marsden's sorts of approach to comprehensivization – the support for the community school. On this conception of the comprehensive school, the catchment area is supposed to be the whole of the immediate neighbourhood of the school. The curriculum would be radically changed to involve study and action on community problems and the free use of the school by the local community would be encouraged. Apart from the rather restricted range of neighbourhoods in which this kind of school would be appropriate, it does not seem to me that this conception of the school as a self-help social work agency would achieve much beyond relieving local authorities and central government of some of their responsibility for welfare provision. But the general idea at work here, that education can be an instrument for social reform, is, and has been, widespread in Social Democratic circles. Yet proposals, for instance, that the methods and content of education would be used to instil socialist values – co-operation, altruism, autonomy – whilst often very radical in appearance and intent, involve a very fundamental misconception about the relationships between ideologies and other aspects of social reality. (See M. Parkinson, op. cit., n. 6, p. 21: 'The annual Conference urged the creation of a specifically working-class education which would develop socialist values, substituting co-operation for competition amongst children and other qualities and outlooks essential to a citizen of a co-operative commonwealth. . . .') The assumption is that working class children, fully equipped in terms of values and attitudes for life in a socialist society would, once let loose in a capitalist society, proceed to transform it into a socialist one. Now, whilst the notion that ideologies have real and important effects in society underlies much of what I have written, it does not follow that the transition to socialism can be effected by an ideological change alone. Ideologies, to be sustained at all, must be sufficiently adequate to the real world to provide the basis for at least *some* adequacy in negotiating it. Our co-operative and altruistic children would soon become more bloody-minded after a few months' exposure to life on the factory floor. To explain precisely why this is so would be a long and difficult task, but at least the first outlines of an explanation can be sketched. We can distinguish two aspects within what I have called the reproduction of capitalist social relationships: the reproduction of *positions* (including occupational), and the reproduction of the *agents* who fill them. Although education primarily carries out the latter function, it is the *former* which plays the dominant role in the over-all reproduction of capitalist social relations (see Poulantzas, 1973, pp. 49/50). A related point is made by A. E. Jenning (*The Struggle in Education*, p. 34): '. . . university expansion has not produced more jobs for graduates, rather more jobs for graduates had produced university expansion, and a fall in their rate of increase has produced more graduate bus conductors.'

The last of current labour education thought, which I shall take up briefly, is the notion of the educational process as one in which the full potentialities of the individual are brought out and developed. This may, one day, form one of the ideological bases for a socialist educational practice, but advocated as an educational principle under capitalism it is quite as utopian as the previous suggestion. This is brought out quite clearly in some versions which come very close to asserting a pre-established harmony between the distribution of individual potentialities in a population and the requirements of the capitalist economic system. This assumption is very clearly present in *The Red Paper*, Cuddihy, Gowan, Lindsay, p. 3:

People used to talk – some still do – as though personal development is one thing and socially necessary skills another. Actually both are components in a single dynamic. A child whose confidence and curiosity are constantly fostered *wants* to acquire the skills he sees in his society, and is prepared to apply the effort necessary to do so. If he does not, then either he lacks the confidence necessary to risk the failure of the attempt; or his experience of life, and his perspective on society, are so faulty that he does not understand the relevance of the skills.

In other words: adjust yourselves, there can't be a fault in reality.

This notion of education as the full flowering of individual potentialities also has an anarchist version – the work of Ivan Illich providing a good example. This version is much more sophisticated than the Social Democratic one and *contrasts* education, as depicted above, with schooling, the practice which goes under the misnomer of education. On this perspective, personal development can only be achieved by dismantling the schools: deschool society. The trouble here, again, of course is that this process is thought of as occurring within the framework of capitalist society. Illich even speaks of encouraging capitalist enterprises to divert finances from advertising towards providing educational facilities for the public on the premises (Illich, 1971, p. 88). Illich's characterizations of the function of the educational system in advanced capitalist societies are confused, metaphorical and eclectic, but it seems that he sees schools as functioning mainly to turn their inmates into happy consumers of the commodities which capitalist societies worship. In technically advanced societies, the production of commodities requires less devotion of human labour than the production of *demand* for them – hence the expansion of the education industry. The idea is that, somehow, the rejection of schooling can lead to the

B

rejection of consumption as a way of life, and so to the destruction of capitalism itself.

First, these notions involve an absurd overestimation of the ideological role of the school system in determining future patterns of consumption. In so far as they have any significant function in this respect it is through the effects of schooling on the future incomes of their pupils. This, in turn, is largely a function of the position of those pupils in the system of production. Secondly, and following from this, Illich's strategy for social transformation gives altogether too much significance to the market, underestimating the fundamental determining role of production. In short, Illich seems to suppose that we are all stuck with capitalism because we are so hooked on commodities. The truth, however, is close to the reverse of this.

I have been attempting to criticize some ideological notions about education and its relations to the rest of society, and to point out some of the political errors to which they lead. In the course of this criticism I have attempted to build up an alternative theoretical account, and I shall end with a few words about the political directions in which this alternative account points.

In these very brief remarks my main concern is the direction to be taken by those – students, teachers, school pupils – who are involved in struggles within the educational system, and who, in one way or another, see socialism as the ultimate goal of their struggles. The first point is that the conception of the state – and of the educational system as an apparatus of the state – which I have been expounding does not make a political strategy which relies centrally on the electoral victory of a Social Democratic Party seem a very promising one. As the recent tragic events in Chile show, for a left-wing party – or alliance of parties – to form a government on the basis of an electoral victory is by no means the same thing as capturing state power.

The other institutions of the state (administrative bureaucracy, army, police, etc.) may continue to function, as before, in the interests of the ruling class.

After the experience of 1964–70, that these remarks apply to the Labour party (even if returned with socialist policies) may not be very controversial. But the most powerful alternative force on the left, the Communist party, also bases its strategy on electoral victory, in alliance with a left-dominated Labour party. However, its understanding of the state, though defective, is more sophisticated than that of the Labour party, so that a full critique of the parliamentary road as an overall strategy would have to give special attention to the Communist party's distinctive version of it. (Reading on this question could usefully begin with the programme of the Communist Party of Great Britain, *The British Road to Socialism* and Bill Warren's criticisms of it in *New Left Review*, 63, Sept./Oct. 1973, p. 27.) Equally, the various struggles in the name of participation and democracy in education, which call for partnership with the agencies of state power in implementing educational policy, suffer from similar illusions about the nature of the state. Indeed, plans for making education democratic also form part of the Communist party's own programme, together with a more radical version of Labour's reorganization policies – full comprehensivization and an end to fee-paying.

The only realistic alternative to these strategies is to attempt to form alliances both within the various structures of the educational system, and between those fighting within education and other oppressed or exploited classes and strata. The central axis of all these alliances must be the working class, as the only class with the strategic position and the organizational possibilities to play the leading role in such a struggle, but it is equally important to recognize the relative autonomy and indispensibility of the various struggles in education. In other words, it is important to recognize that teachers, pupils, students and workers are *not* parts of the same class, but have different and sometimes contradictory interests. This point is not fully recognized by either of the main Marxist organizations – International Socialists and International Marxist Group – active in educational politics to the left of the Communist party. Jenning (*The Struggle in Education*, p. 36) says that conflicts between pupils and teachers are 'conflicts within the working class as a whole', whilst Rosenberg (*Education and Society*, p. 22) also includes teachers as part of the working class. Rosenberg actually manages to combine this with the view that teachers are also agents of the ruling class (p. 21) and that attacks on teachers by working class children can be instances of class struggle.

In fact, however, teachers do not relate to working class children simply as agents of the ruling class, but nor are they part of the working class themselves. The political problem for the left within the teachers' and students' unions is *not* to attempt to rectify a mysteriously mistaken sense of class identity but to forge an *alliance*, on the basis of both analysis and struggle, between strata with distinct interests. Such an alliance is possible only on the condition that the contradictions between these groups are secondary in relation to the contradictions between them all and the ruling class. Even then a great deal needs to be done both by way of thorough analysis of the concrete situation in which we are working and political action to establish a common basis for struggle. To some extent this is a question of bringing together organizationally and theoretically many individual achievements and fragmented struggles. Rank and File's encouragement of the formation of school and student unions, some important cases of trade union action in defence of victimized militants in education, the use of university facilities for flying-pickets during the miners' strike, and for other purposes in solidarity with workers' struggles – these are just a few of the concrete achievements which now have to be built upon.

Reading Guide

Althusser, L., 'Ideology and Ideological State Apparatuses', in *Lenin and Philosophy and other Essays*, New Left Books, London 1971

Blackburn, R., *Ideology in Social Science*, Fontana 1972

Blackburn and Cockburn, *The Incompatibles*, Penguin 1967

Communist Party of Great Britain, *The British Road to Socialism*

Engels, F., *The Origins of the Family, Private Property and the State* (various editions)

Ford, J., *Social Class and the Comprehensive School*, Routledge and Kegan Paul 1969

Goldthorpe, Lockwood, Bechhofer and Platt, *The Affluent Worker: Political Attitudes and Behaviour*, Cambridge 1968

Hindess, B., *The Decline of Working Class Politics*, Merlin 1971

Illich, I. D., *Deschooling Society*, Penguin 1971

Jenning, A. E., *The Struggle in Education*, IMG Publications 1972

Lenin, V. I., *The State and Revolution* (various editions)

Marsden, D., *Politicians, Equality and the Comprehensives*, Fabian Tract 4III

Parkinson, M., *The Labour Party and the Organisation of Secondary Education 1918–65*, Routledge and Kegan Paul 1970

Poulantzas, N., *Political Power and Social Classes*, New Left Books, and Shead and Ward 1973

Poulantzas, N., *Marxism and Social Classes*, New Left Books 78

Rosenberg, C., *Education and Society*, Rank and File Teachers pamphlet

Rubinstein and Stoneman, *Education for Democracy*, Penguin (2nd edition) 1972

2. Economists and 'Human Capital'

Adam Westoby

If the political groups have generally failed to understand the true nature of educational politics, economists have had even less success in coming to grips with the educational process. This is mainly due to the inverted nature of much economic thinking itself. Adam Westoby indicates how, instead of enlightening us, economists tend to spread confusion with notions such as 'human capital' – as if the process of human learning can be reduced to acquiring commodities.

Adam Westoby was born in 1944. He went to Oxford University and now lectures on education at the Open University.

What the economics of education makes clear is that modern economics, more than in any preceding period, separates and insulates in its theories various spheres of society and gives an account of them which suggests that they can, at least in some sense, be objectively understood as subject to their own laws and limited to their own field of action. This is one aspect of the characteristic of thought which Lukacs describes under the general heading of reification. (See *History and Class Consciousness*, London 1968, especially pp. 103 *et. seq.*) It is, as he described it, the tendency toward mental separation, abstraction, and the disintegration in consciousness of many of the relationships which exist in reality, this tendency being the reflection in thought of commodity production as a universal feature of society.

The economics of education – by which I mean that body of economic theory which tries to bring the process of education and its consequences within its own theories of exchange value – has a large, and ever expanding, literature. It may soon be a full-time job just to read all that is being written. I have, therefore, had to find a more limited volume of material which epitomizes the subject as a whole, and I have in fact selected one book: Professor Blaug's *An Introduction to the Economics of Education* (Penguin 1970), in the bibliography of which are to be found almost all but the most recent central references. But the subject will not, from a scientific point of view, be of any permanent importance. If the economics of education and its associated theories of human capital catch our attention, they do so not as a renaissance or new departure, but as the final flowering of a tradition that has already outlived its years of strength. For the future historian of style in bourgeois economic thought, the economics of education will fall firmly within the roccoco period. If we turn to the subject, it is only in the spirit of Goethe's remark that 'to attain to truth it is necessary to drain the cup of error to the dregs'.

In fact the economists of education do us a signal service in distilling the ideological essence contained within the general body of modern bourgeois economics. Before this point can emerge more than abstractly, however, we must briefly sketch the history of the economics of education and mention some of the main logical and methodological objections to it.

During the 1950s a number of economists, particularly in the United States and Western Europe, began to remark that the average earning of workers with more years of schooling are higher than those with fewer years. In part, of course, this was to be explained by their greater ability, their different racial and geographical composition and the supposedly stronger motivations of those who travelled further through the educational system. However, having made, in various studies, statistical corrections for the influence of such factors, they concluded that at least a part of the additional earnings were attributable to additional education (the widely adopted fraction is two-thirds, known as Dennison's alpha-coefficient). Now, as any well-behaved student of bourgeois economics knows, all income must have a source-cum-recipient, and the basic sources of income in the modern economy are labour and capital. How then are the higher earnings of educated labour to be explained? Naturally by the supposition that these workers carry embodied in them various quantities of capital, not ordinary capital but human capital. How is this capital created? Well, it is the economic end-product of the education system, its output.

It is important to note that this rather brief argument serves to bring the economics of education firmly into the fold of neo-classical economics – i.e. the mainstream of modern bourgeois economics, of which the basic framework is that the prices of goods, and the quantity produced are determined by supply and demand. It is even more important to notice one crucial stage involved on the way. This is the assumption that differences of income must as a general rule reflect differences of social productivity. It is of the essence of neo-classical economics to deny any separability of the process of social production from that of the distribution of the social product.

Having brought the subject within the general ambit of neo-classical economics, the way was set clear for a proliferation of algebraically elaborate theories on the processes whereby human capital is produced and employed. (These theories of human capital must be clearly distinguished from the various non-economic techniques of *manpower planning* which have been developed over the same period, but which do not involve any *theoretical* account of the prices of different grades of labour – i.e. of relative wages and salaries – and therefore can take no account of changes in these prices.)

At least two factors have given these theories a more ethereal flavour than the generality of economics. The first is the particular character of human capital. As its name implies it is inextricably connected with individual human beings, and in civilized societies human beings are not bought and sold. They are, as the jurist quaintly has it, inalienable. As a consequence human capital cannot itself appear on the market and acquire an observable price. What is bought and sold is the flow of its services. This, however, is always sold as a joint good with labour. Human capital therefore never appears as an ordinary commodity on the market. Its value must, consequently, be indirectly measured. It is therefore apparent that the quantitative concept of human capital will have an inbuilt tendency to imprecision.

The second, connected, reason is that education is universally admitted to have other effects besides increasing the earnings of individuals. Moreover, it is undertaken by individuals for motives which are not limited to the expectation that by submitting themselves to a course of education they will increase their earnings in the future. Both these aspects of the processes of education, broadly speaking, the sociological and psychological ones, have effects and repercussions in many areas of society. These effects include effects upon the productivity of both other workers and of non-human means of production.

By referring in this way to such a wealth of social events we are forced to give a near-caricature of the process of education in society. But the neo-classical economist, on

the other hand, has no such scruples as to simplification.
As far as he is concerned all these effects can be assimilated to economic effects: the device for such assimilation
is known in the trade as 'externalities'. Anyone familiar
with the variety of items to which prices may be imputed by
economists would not be surprised to know that many
things besides the monetary and direct resource costs of
education, and the additional earnings of the educated, have
been thrown into the scales of cost-benefit analysis. An
illustrative list would include: the increased degree of civic
responsibility in the population which results from higher
education, and the consequent possibilities for reducing the
law-and-order budget; the release of married women and
their associated marginal productivities into the labour
force due to the child-minding functions of nurseries; the
savings resulting from most men in a developed economy
being able to fill out their own tax forms, and so on.

This approach – reducing the most qualitatively diverse
social, psychological and historical phenomena to a single,
common, quantative denominator – is of course not pecu-
liar to the economics of education. It occurs also, for
example, in the economics of health, of pollution and the
environment, of transport, communications, and so on.
But what is unique is the extent of false abstraction
achieved in relation to education. For while it is true that
the consciousness formed and transmitted within the
formal educational system of bourgeois society is impoverished, still the process of education, in *any* society, is
par excellence the area in which conscious, subjective, and
qualitative aspects of the total social process are most
concentrated; in which they are distilled, transmuted and
acquired by new generations. Any attempt, therefore, to
calculate, add up, and compare on a *purely quantitative*
basis a range of phenomena whose importance consists
precisely in their qualities, and in the contradictions of

those qualities, is almost guaranteed to scale new heights in the history of mystification. The notion, to take just two examples, that *any part* of the social importance of a tear-gas bio-chemist, or a high court judge, is usefully described by the relationship of their earnings to any other wage or salary figures is evidently more than bizarre.

However, the boundaries and barriers established by what we earlier called reified consciousness are not absolutely fixed. On the contrary, they are in a continual state of tension and motion; intellectuals, and particularly specialized intellectuals, are always coming across things which they cannot – and to do them justice, usually do not wish to – ignore, but which cut across the boundaries of their separated disciplines. The attempt to grasp these theoretically must clearly tend to force alterations within theoretical consciousness.

Thus the economics of education, which only began to develop on a wide scale after pressure from the middle and working classes had obliged the state apparatuses of the developed capitalist countries to spend rapidly increasing sums on free or subsidized mass education, is an example of one particular compartment of reified consciousness attempting to extend, both quantitatively and qualitatively, the limits of its subject matter, but without making any substantial alteration to the limits of its methodology.

Only from this standpoint and not from the individual eccentricities of its practitioners, is it possible to understand its strange features. These are, indeed, various. Blaug's *An Introduction to the Economics of Education* contains a useful selection. It has recently been published as a paperback, and seems likely to go some way towards becoming a widely read and used textbook – an additional reason for devoting some attention to it.

On the first page, under the heading 'Human Capital: Metaphor or Analogy?', we read:

in all economies of which we have knowledge, people with
more education earn on average higher incomes than people
with less education. . . . Thus, in this very simple sense, the costs
incurred by individuals in acquiring more education constitute
an investment in their own future earning capacity. (p. 1)

and the next paragraph continues:

But surely this is not the principal reason that students stay on
in school after the legal school leaving age? Were any of us
aware of life-time earnings prospects when we decided to acquire
O-level or A-levels? Probably not. What we did was to take the
advice of our parents that 'it would be a good thing', or simply
imitated our friends who were no doubt being advised by their
parents along similar lines. And why did our parents consider it
'a good thing'? Because everyone knows that 'you need more
education nowadays to get a good job'. And translated into the
language of economists: 'because education nowadays is a
profitable private investment'. We do not have to assume fully
conscious motivation or perfect knowledge of the distribution of
earnings by age and educational qualifications. Nor do we need
to ignore all other motives for staying on in school. All that is
required is the idea that the higher earnings of educated people
is a significant element in the demand for education. (p. 1)

The relationship of this economic parable with psychological theory is here already stretched. By page 171, it is
severed altogether:

The private rate of return on investment in education reduces
the first pair of cost-benefit streams to a single number. The
yield of the best alternative investment option available to
households likewise reduces the second pair to a single number,
ignoring for the moment what yield in the real world corresponds to it. The decision criterion is: remain at school if the
private rate of return on the next increment of education exceeds
the yield of the best alternative investment option, and not
otherwise. In other words, we are assuming that people acquire
extra education only when the job opportunities and the associated life-time income stream that it is expected to create out-

weigh the value of the time and resources that will have to be invested, due allowance being made for the fact that income foregone in the present is worth more than equivalent income accruing in the future. Rigorously expressed, we are postulating the existence of a rational educational calculus according to which students or their parents act *as if* they were equalizing rates of return on all possible investment options available to them. (p. 171)

We should notice that Blaug is now quite unconcerned with the actual, profane thoughts of individual human beings. According to him a 'rational educational calculus' is in operation only provided that students or their parents act *as if* they were equalizing rates of return.

Now, if they merely act *as if*, it is possible that their reasoning involves quite other factors, or none, or that their behaviour is not based on their reasoning at all. So at this point we are to understand that the anecdotal material provided earlier in the book was not intended as evidence, but solely as a form of metaphoric illustration. According to Blaug, it is not that such conversations between parents and children actually *do* or need take place, but that they *would* if only people's rationality was developed to the point where they thought they were doing those things which, in point of fact, they are doing.

From this it seems that Blaug's account of the conscious behaviour of individuals requires one of two more or less equally naive psychological theories:

(a) what we might call the tactile empiricist, or pudding is in the eating, view, according to which motives are those which agents – i.e. anyone apart from deviants – *would* have had if they were behaving rationally; or alternatively,

(b) a doctrine of universal or divine reason (already unfashionable, I am sorry to say, even in the most intellectually leisurely of British universities) according to which the necessary behaviour of individuals – including, of course, their participation in the labour market – follows the most categorical of imperatives, the pursuit of cash, and is quite independent of whatever contingent happenings may be going on in the space between their ears.

That Blaug is not completely unconscious of these objections becomes clear in the next paragraph, which begins 'Put like that it sounds absurd'. But even this generous admission offers us little basis for agreement with him. For what he means by absurd is something relatively superficial: that the abstracted picture he is putting forward is clearly at odds with reality. But there is a deeper, and more serious, absurdity to the theory. What is striking about it is the attempt to reduce every element in the economy to the rational, anonymous profit-maximizer who forms the basic animal and essential building block of the neoclassical economic universe. In a precisely similar vein the individual in general is traditionally treated in the elementary textbooks as a utility-maximizer and the algebraic treatment of his behaviour is identical with that used in the theory of the firm. In essence we are being told that every unit of the economy, from General Motors to the man in the street, participates in the process of social production in the same way, i.e. by sliding gaily up and down a pair of supply and demand curves. Ideology has here reached the point that the capitalist class (and its intellectual representatives), try as it may to study social reality, can see nothing beyond its own image. This is perhaps why Blaug introduces his account of the economics of education under capitalism with an eight-page discussion of the economics of slavery – a slave society being one in which human capital can be marketed and its price reported from day to day in the financial press. The full gamut of marginal economics, including the assumption of an organized capital and financial market, is brought into play together with the simplifying assumption that marketed stocks of labour and human capital are provided through the institution of chattel slavery. If this were nothing more than a modelling device, intended only to abstract from some institutional restriction on the universal presence of the market economy, there would be less wrong with it. But Blaug's discussion is, in fact, liberally peppered with empirical and historical observations on the actual history of slavery: in ancient Greece and Rome and in the pre-Civil War American South.

A similar all-pervasive use of economic concepts is involved in the section on education as consumption and investment. This is a relevant subject since, as a fair number of teachers are aware, *some* students actually enjoy study independently of the higher earnings which will ultimately crown their efforts. Having reviewed various views of the distinction between investment and consumption (and hazarded some remarks on national income accounting), Blaug arrives at the position that:

the contrast between consumption and investment depends on who it is that makes the decision to purchase, rather than on the type of good that is being purchased. (p. 17)

This, one might hope, contains a germ of social realism, but the hope proves shortlived. For the social identity of the 'who' deciding on purchases turns out to depend on psychology, and this, as we have already seen, is a matter on which Blaug is agnostic.

Thus he continues:

For example, a 'household' decides to acquire an additional year of schooling for one of its younger members. This is 'consumption' in the Keynesian world. But it turns out that the additional schooling renders the member of the household more productive once he enters the labour force. This makes it 'investment' according to the classical definition. Unfortunately, both the student and his parents are unaware that additional education acts to increase the future productivity and hence the life-time earnings expectations of the student. This makes it 'consumption' again, at least if our definition emphasizes the personal motive for an expenditure; from a social point of view, however, it remains in part 'investment'. Thus, the definition of consumption and investment changes as the angle of vision does. (p. 19)

The difficulty is severe, since we are required to make important distinctions on the basis of facts about which we can have little or no knowledge. The solution cannot be described as satisfactory, even though it employs an honoured device in the British intellectual tradition: compromise. Blaug concludes:

It is useful to think of a three-fold category rather than a two-fold one: education may be acquired by individuals as if it were (a) a non-durable consumer good, (b) a durable consumer good and (c) a capital good. (p. 20)

This multiplication of categories gives the clearest expression to the type of abstraction involved. For neo-classical economists the interrelationships of commodities, and the social interrelationships of human beings which lie behind them, are reduced to three categories of package deals in utility – having all your happiness now and none later, some now and some later, and all of it later. As Blaug remarks in his preface: 'We do not need to know a great deal of economics to apply it to education, but the little we do know we must have in our bones.' Evidently it is not only hardened enemies of the social fabric who are persuaded of the ossification of intellectual life under capitalism.

But despite all its deficiencies (and very probably because of some of them) the concept of human capital has not stayed within theoretical boundaries. In a developed capitalist state such as post-war Britain, with more or less universal secondary education, ever-increasing staying-on rates beyond the age of compulsory school attendance, and mushrooming applications for higher and fuller full-time education, there is clearly scope for the practical application of the concept to policy making. And the most obvious target is higher education, with different levels, subjects and types of courses continually competing for limited public funds.

In fact, in 1970, the Department of Education and Science, which since the Robbins Report (1963) had used the demand from qualified applicants as the basic criterion for the expansion of higher education, seriously considered 'the rate of return (or investment of human capital) approach' as an alternative. (See Department of Education and Science Education Planning Paper No. 2, *Student Numbers in Higher Education in England and Wales*, HMSO 1970.) It was not then adopted, but the door was by no means shut. The DES maintained that the alternative approaches were, though 'conceptually distinguishable', none the less 'closely intertwined in reality and should not be regarded as independent approaches'. The Planning Paper looked forward to the time when the follow-up survey of earnings, based on the 1966 census, would begin to 'provide material for the fuller use of this technique in improving estimates of society's needs for higher education'.

In fact, since then, a number of economists close to the DES and the Central Statistical Office have published papers giving calculations of the *social* rate of return – i.e. the rate of return using total resource costs, whether borne by the individual or the state, and pre-tax earnings – on the human capital produced by the main qualifications of higher and further education. (See, for example, Morris and Ziderman, *Economic Trends*, 1972.)

Of course, there can be no immediate conversion of the planning mechanisms of higher education, such as they are, to gear the system as a whole to maximizing the overall social rate of return. In addition to all the political and social obstacles to doing this, the method simply is not suitable for wholesale application. The problems involved in collecting the necessary statistical information on the earnings, age and educational history of the population, making the appropriate calculations, and then giving some sort of meaning to the final result, are enormous. And even if a government were satisfied with some set of solutions to these problems, the method faces big obstacles even as a purely operational or pragmatic guide to action. For, even if calculation shows the rate of return to a certain type of education (say mechanical engineering degrees) to be high, and even if one is prepared to conclude from this that there is, in some sense, a shortage of mechanical engineering graduates, one still does not know how large this shortage is or even whether it is growing or diminishing. A rate of return resembles a price in that it is some sort of signal from a blindly operating market. Unlike an ordinary price, however, one cannot observe it on the surface of events, from day to day. Even to detect a trend requires repeated data collection and calculation.

So even for those whose faith in the invisible hand of the market mechanism is unshakeable, rates of return are still very dubious indicators. The only pragmatic advice they can give is: reduce the shortage (or the surplus) a bit, then make the calculation again. But since comparisons of price information over time during inflation are notoriously difficult; since the numbers employed are continually being altered, not only by the input from the education system, but by retirement, death, emigration and immigration, marriage and so on; and since provision for education needs to be planned and buildings constructed some years in advance – it is inconceivable that calculations of return on human capital could ever become more than the blind leading the blind. And in a decentralized education system like Britain's this would be doubly the case.

But, as history and common observation confirm, the fact that a course of action is irrational provides no guarantee that it will not be adopted. British capitalism in the 1970s faces an economic and political crisis in which it must, by hook or by crook, try to break the strength of the organized working class, and make a major shift in the distribution of income away from wages and in favour of profits. In this situation the education reforms of the post-war period are clearly at risk, since education spending is now the largest and one of the fastest-growing components of public expenditure. The 1972 education White Paper (DES, *Education: A Framework for Expansion*, HMSO 1972) concentrated in the post-secondary sector on cost cutting and staffing economies; if the calculation of returns is to be used directly in policy decisions, it will most likely be to decide the first victims of containment and cut-backs in full-time higher education.

But the central interest of the concept of human capital, as of bourgeois economics as a whole, does not lie in the extent to which it may be pressed into service in attempts to control a social system which is fundamentally anarchic. Its essential significance is in the light it throws on the way that class society *inverts* human consciousness so that it reflects social reality as fixed, conservative abstractions which obliterate the wealth and movement of the real world.

But this being said, it must also be said that it is very rare (in fact virtually impossible) to find any economist, whatever his political or philosophical persuasions, who would explicitly deny that the interconnections of the education system with the economy and with the whole of the rest of society are both intimate and complex. It is thus only a preliminary criticism to point to the existence of all sorts of such connections.

There is, however, one form of abstraction which we have already mentioned and which lies at the very heart of neo-classical economics, and of human capital theories. This is the separation of the problem of distribution of the total social product from the ensemble of antagonisms and connections which make up the overall relations of the social classes. This particular form of abstraction occurs in an inverted form within economics, namely, as the *apparent integration* of the problems of distribution and production; so that the return on capital, physical or human, appears as a reward for its contribution to production. So two birds are killed with one stone. On the one hand, the capitalist class is divested of its role as an exploiting and ruling class, with all the political, judicial, psychological and educational processes in which this is expressed. It is provided with an entirely opposite description as the vehicle of an indispensible factor of production: capital. Then, as an ironic afterthought, a certain fraction of this social mass of capital is theoretically donated to the working population to explain differences in the productivity of individual workers.

In fact the notion of capital defined as a factor of production has prompted a violent controversy – over aggregation problems – within bourgeois economics itself in the last decade (for a useful introduction see Harcourt, G. C., *Some Cambridge Controversies in the Theory of Capital,* 1972). Crudely and abstractly put the central problem of neo-classical economics is that it seeks to reconcile and harmonize two fundamentally antagonistic characteristics of capitalist society – the socialized character of production, and the individual nature of appropriation. It is this which provides the contradictory core of the way in which man's intercourse with nature is conducted through, and in conflict with, his social relations with himself in capitalist society. The economists encounter their apparently technical problems because for them it is an unconscious article of faith that the economic behaviour of an individual may be understood independently of the social relations in which he is involved, and the history of these social relations. They *first* describe the essence of economic man as an isolated individual, and *then* they bring him into association with other men. The difficulties involved in so doing are referred to as aggregation problems. But this is to misunderstand them. Over a century ago Marx explained that man, as the object of knowledge, could not be considered as squatting outside society. He *necessarily* appears to the scientist as already formed by his social relations. Marx's study of economics thus provided the occasion for a rich and lengthy exploration of social mankind, and his consciousness, in capitalist society.

It is of central importance to notice that the aggregation problems of neo-classical economics do not arise from *ignoring* the facts of social production and individual appropriation. On the contrary, it comes about precisely because these contradictory aspects of capitalist society are built into it. The individual is described as an individual, and in his individual relation to commodities – as a buyer of commodities (demand) and a seller (supply). Microeconomics consists of defining and analysing such an individual in his relation to commodities. The social relations of production are then separately analysed, but in a disguised form as relations between commodities – labour in general and capital in general, in the simplest case. As long as these two spheres are held separate, contradictions are *bound* to arise in the attempt to reconcile them. For, to derive the characteristics of commodities (their relative prices) as they confront the individual man, we must have already discovered the social relations of whole classes. The matter comes to a head in the problem of distribution. For the behaviour of commodities evidently depends on who owns them depends in its turn on how much he owns. And in fact, the price of labour power, and with it the rate of profit and the system of relative prices of commodities, is decided in the course of struggle between the social classes. Prices, thus, are not only decided by the free appearance of commodities on the market, but equally by the withdrawal of one particular commodity – labour power – from the market, in the course of strikes.

The contradiction between individual activity and social relations was analysed by Marx, as is well known, in the form of the contradiction between use value and exchange value within the commodity, in *Capital*. A proper understanding of the significance of the notion of human capital requires us to recapitulate some of the elements of this analysis.

Marx draws a definite distinction between labour power, which he regards as a commodity, and labour, the life activity of social human beings, which is not a commodity. Under capitalism the labourer is separated from the means of production. These are concentrated, as commodities and as capital, in the hands of an opposing class. The means of production, that is to say, appear – not simply as physical objects, but in their social relations – as something set over, and against, the labourer; as a hostile social power. In what sense is capital hostile? Because in order to carry out his own basic life activity as a social human being, labour, the worker must get to grips with the means of production. This he can *only* do, under capitalism, by selling the sole commodity which he possesses – his labour power. The appearance of labour power as a commodity is thus inextricably tied to the social and historical process of separating a propertyless working class from the means of production, themselves first concentrated in the hands of the nascent capitalist class during the process of primitive capitalist accumulation. Here the *logic* of Marx's analysis of the commodity as a universal feature of society reflects the historical process of its birth.

We should notice what an important development Marx is pointing to. History, in his view, is the history of man's struggle to overcome, to achieve freedom over, nature. This struggle is not direct but is mediated through the social relations in which man finds himself. Man advances in this struggle mainly by extending the social character of it, the social division of labour. Education, including the development of a separate social caste of intellectuals, is one aspect of this. But at the point where this socialization of the struggle is *most developed*, it is also *most subordinated* to the social relations. Under capitalism, historical, labouring man can only act upon nature by permission of the market, of the laws of commodities. Man finds himself opposed to nature therefore, not directly, but in and through the commodity, and this contradictory relation is reflected in the dual aspects of *both* labour *and* the commodity. Labour is *both* concrete labour, qualitatively specific (through experience or education) and resulting in specific use values, *and* abstract labour; a social substance, as Marx expresses it, quite without quality and characterized only by its exchangeability, its quantum. This abstract labour gives rise to value.

These two pairs of opposites are inseparably *united* – use value and value within the commodity, and concrete and abstract labour in human activity. The social character of both appears as an independent power set over against the individual worker. This is not merely commodities, but capital. The emergence of labour power as a commodity is not simultaneous with the appearance of commodities as such. The development of commodity production as one form among others preceded by a considerable period of time the emergence of capitalism. Capital, and its concomitant, the appearance of labour power, come into being only as the social power necessary to render the commodity form of production universal. Capital is, however, more than this quantitative universality. It is an independent social force, continually transforming and expanding itself through the circulation of commodities. Just as labour is permitted to occur only through entering into the circulation of commodities, commodities themselves occur under capitalism only as one phase in the life-cycle of capital.

Not only is the appearance of labour power as a commodity the necessary condition of capital, it is also a prerequisite for the appearance of political economy. Only when abstract, dead, labour had made itself apparent could man begin to analyse social production as an overall process. To do so it was necessary to abstract from the qualitative variety of the labour process, and to see it as taking place in accordance with the laws of commodity circulation, and above those, the laws of capital accumulation.

It is at this point that we can begin to glimpse the shallowness of the notion of human capital. Unable to understand human activity other than as the exchange of commodities, the culminating form of the commodity – capital – is dragooned into service to provide an account of the most qualitatively diverse of human activities, the conscious process of learning, knowing and acting in the world. Not only this, but the notion of capital employed is a *purely* quantitative one.

Why, then, *do* more educated workers have higher incomes than those with less education? In large part because a high proportion of the more educated sections of the labour force are not employed in the *creation* of surplus value, and they perform tasks which, by and large, are concerned with the organization and enforcement of the process of social production, with the realization of values in the market, and with the political and ideological maintenance of capitalism. In a society where commodity production is generalized, many things which are not commodities nonetheless acquire a price. The genteel expression of this process is so-called welfare economics, the actual expression is the widespread corruption of human motives. The presumption that graduates earn more than other men because they have more human capital is only slightly less nonsensical than the supposition that the earnings of the bishop, the prostitute, or the professor of economics reflect their contributions to the social process of creating wealth.

Reading Guide

An Introduction to the Economics of Education by Mark Blaug (Allen Lane, The Penguin Press 1970) is a standard textbook on the economics of education, which explains and defends the concept of human capital.

Some Cambridge Controversies in the Theory of Capital by G. C. Harcourt (Cambridge University Press 1972) summarizes the attack (mainly by neo-Ricardians) on neoclassical theories of capital and (by implication) therefore of human capital.

3. Language and Class

Harold Rosen

Just as the nature of class domination and its relation to education is usually misunderstood, so the nature of the working class and its experience in schools is usually misrepresented. In particular it has become fashionable to explain the dominated situation of working class pupils in terms of some characteristic or other of these young people themselves. They are seen as failing in one way or another. Most recently it is their language which has been singled out for attention as causing them to fail in school. Harold Rosen exposes the fallacy of this type of approach by a critical analysis of the views of one sociologist whose notion of 'linguistic codes' is now accepted as fact by many teachers.

Harold Rosen is at present a Senior Lecturer in Education in the English Department of the University of London Institute of Education. Previously he taught in a variety of secondary schools and was head of the English Department at a London comprehensive. In addition to being involved in teacher education he has spent a number of years in research into the written language. He is joint author, with his wife, of The Language of Primary School Children *(Penguin), and with Douglas Barnes and James Britton of* Language, the Learner and the School *(Penguin).*

This essay has appeared separately as a pamphlet published by Falling Wall Press in 1972.

. . . lower-lower class parental patterns, compared to middle class ones, tend to be antithetical to a child's positive mental health . . . With generally less ego strength (lower self-esteem), the very poor individual is apt to have greater need than his middle class counterpart for security-giving psychological defenses . . . The subcultural patterns of this group . . . suggest that their life style . . . might be termed (within the middle class frame of reference), as immature in a number of respects, such as their greater tendency toward impulsivity, lack of goal commitment, magical thinking, physical learning and behavioral styles, low frustration tolerance, concrete attitudes, and so on. (from Chilman, *Growing up Poor*, quoted in Ryan, 1971)

The jargon is contemporary but the matter familiar. For well over a century there has been an uninterrupted flow of scholars, philanthropists, politicians and others who contemplated the working class and were far from pleased with what they saw. There are innumerable accounts of fecklessness, improvidence, laziness, immorality, violence and tendencies to mob behaviour and riot. More recently, a considerable body of scholars, particularly in the United States, has exercised its expensive skills to show among other things that compared with the middle class (its own class) the working class bring up their children in an unsatisfactory manner with dire consequences for their subsequent success at school. By these means we are offered the central explanation of why the working class (or, as the jargon has it, the 'culturally deprived', the 'disadvantaged', the 'underprivileged') fail to learn in our schools in spite of our tireless efforts to educate them. As the scholarly scrutiny of the life habits of the working class proceeds, more and more attention has focused upon their language (which as everyone knows distinguishes them from others much more effectively than, say, horny hands and overalls). In a wide range of publications and researches, psychologists, linguists and sociologists have in a short space of time turned their attention to a subject which, in spite of its ready accessibility, they had been content to leave to such marginal characters as folk-lorists (dismissed as romantics), dialectologists (dismissed as mere linguistic cartographers) and novelists (not accepted as sources of evidence). Around this theme a debate has finally emerged precisely because on the one hand there are honest and devoted people who are trying to answer the question, 'Why do so many working class children fail in school and how can we change things so that they do not?'; and on the other hand because there are people who, in the effort to guard their privileges and power within the education system, seek tirelessly for new and better theoretical justifications – if need be, adapting and vulgarizing in the process. At the storm centre of the debate stands the work of Basil Bernstein which advances theories that claim to lay bare critical relationships between class, language and educability. It would be difficult to exaggerate the extent to which his ideas have received acceptance throughout the educational world and well beyond it, so much so that they are always referred to with deference at the level of professorial debate and the terms 'restricted' and 'elaborated' codes have entered the folk-lore of classroom teachers.

There are two interesting features to the almost unanimous acceptance of these ideas (there are a few notable exceptions, one of which I shall refer to later). The first is that both right and left in education politics have seen in these ideas support for their views. Thus Bantock (1965) on the right justifies separate education for working class children and cites Bernstein in support, and Brian Jackson (1968) on the left accepts the main thesis. Jensen (1968) cites Bernstein in the very same paragraph in which he makes the outrageous statement that 'much of working-class language consists of a kind of "emotional" accompaniment to action here and now'.

This support from two opposed sides (many other examples could be cited) must mean that either someone (or everyone) has got it wrong, or that there are central ambiguities and unresolved contradictions in Bernstein's papers, so that like the Scriptures they can be quoted by the Devil, red or black.

Secondly, and more importantly, the way in which Bernstein's theories have permeated contemporary educational thinking and have been used to justify educational practices is a rare phenomenon in English education and calls for some explanation. Educational academics can weave theories and publish researches to their hearts' content, and these can accumulate over decades, without affecting practice one iota or causing a ripple in staffroom discussion. But there are notable and significant exceptions.

In the fifties the one theory, with its practical application, which touched the lives of every child and teacher in the public system was the prevailing theory of intelligence and the concept of the Intelligence Quotient. It was, above all, educational academics who disseminated the ideas, developed the tests and even at times administered their application to secondary school selection, the 'eleven-plus' tests (Vernon, 1957). However, by the end of the decade both the operation of the system and its underlying theory had been seriously challenged and, in the eyes of many, totally discredited. This opposition came in the main from teachers and from the political left, and was closely connected with the campaign for comprehensive schools (Simon, 1953). They were alerted to the need to challenge the theory when they saw how it offered an apparently cast-iron scientific case for an elitism which could in the political climate of the fifties no longer be taken as self-evident.

It was just when this theory was looking sadly tattered and when the high priest of the psychometric ideology himself, Professor Vernon, felt obliged to publish a self-critical restatement of his position (Vernon, 1960) that the theories of Bernstein began to be available. These early papers, which he himself now says 'were conceptually weak and . . . horrifyingly coarse' (Bernstein, 1971, p. 11) and which were the only ones available for several years, were readily seized upon, not only because of the great upsurge of interest in linguistics, but also because they seemed to offer theoretical respectability to the widespread notion among teachers and others that an intrinsic feature of working class language, rooted in their way of life, disqualified working class children educationally and, by the same token, justified the notion of the superior educational potential of the middle class. Whereas in the fifties children had their IQs branded on their forehead, in the sixties more and more of them had the brand changed to 'restricted' or 'elaborated'. The ideology vacuum had been filled. Moreover, it had been filled at the very moment when the traditional denigration of working class language was totally demolished by much of the work in linguistics which was coming to fruition at this time. No serious writer could go on asserting that working class speech was ungrammatical, lazy, debased and so forth. Bernstein's theories made it possible to bypass all that and to suggest a much more profound and intractable deficiency. The language of the working class was 'restricted', not in the sense that it was 'non-standard' but in the sense that it could not reach out to certain kinds of meanings and limited the power of speakers to understand their environment. The theories pointed to a basic cognitive defect.

Bernstein protests that his work has been misunderstood, misused and vulgarized, just as the psychometrists did before him. And he is absolutely right. However, as he also tells us his papers are 'obscure, lack precision and probably abound in ambiguities' (Bernstein, 1971, p. 19), that is scarcely to be wondered at.

I shall, therefore, in advancing certain criticisms, concentrate on the most recent of the papers selected for publication together last year – those papers, in fact, which present the most developed version of the work that has been going on for over a decade. These are: *A Sociolinguistic Approach to Socialization with some Reference to Educability* (1971), *Social Class, Language and Socialization* (1971), and *A Critique of the Concept of Compensatory Education* (1969) – now available as Chapters 8, 9 and 10 of *Class, Codes and Control*, Vol. 1 (Bernstein, 1971).

Let me now attempt to explain those concepts on which most of the discussion focuses, namely elaborated and restricted codes. I must admit before I set about it that I do not find the task an easy one. These concepts and the theoretical apparatus in which they find a place have been constantly reworked, redefined and explicated. Some have been totally abandoned, others disappear and reappear so that it is difficult to know what is essential and what is marginal.* Moreover, the level of unrelieved abstraction at which the work is pitched makes it difficult to be certain at times to what reality they refer. Nevertheless, in spite of all the shifts of emphasis, redefinitions and qualifications the central concepts of the codes and the main supporting rationale have been sufficiently consistent to permit a summary.

The Bernstein Theory

The thesis states that there is a fundamental qualitative difference between working class (or at least unskilled

---

* For example, in the early work the definition of codes is linked to *predictability*. The Introduction to *Class, Codes and Control* states that this notion of predictability was abandoned because it 'can be given little statistical significance'. It reappears in a very recent paper (1971), in that same volume.

working class)* speech and middle class speech; and that this is not a matter of underlying grammar, dialect or slang, but rather of the different *use* of the grammatical system and vocabulary. The difference will arise from different relationships to the social structure. The two classes can be said to be using different *codes* because there are differences in the principles which underlie the particular choices they make in speech. They arise because there are two different kinds of socialization involved which find their expression in different kinds of language. Children thus acquire different kinds of cultural identity and different responses to that identity. Thus they come to perceive different orders of relevance and relation, of understanding of themselves, others and the world. The class basis of these differences lies in differences in the main socializing agencies, the relationships to family, peer group, school and work. In practice, Bernstein focuses his attention on the family, which he discusses at some length, since it is seen as the microcosm of the operation of class. In neither his theoretical papers nor his research is there an attempt to examine or analyse the role of language in the other spheres – though, as we shall see, he does make statements about them from time to time. Because of the different ways in which the language codes are used, the middle class families are given a sense that the world is permeable and are introduced to the principles of intellectual change, whereas the working class families are not.

How are the two codes that give rise to such dramatic differences described?

(a) The restricted code is highly predictable since it draws on narrow resources of language. Thus it is rigid, whereas the elaborated code is flexible.

* Bernstein says that the unskilled working class are 29 per cent of the population.

(b) In the restricted code the speaker has difficulty in verbalizing his intent, while the middle class speaker finds it easier to verbalize his subjectivity – sociologically, intellectually and affectively.

(c) The codes give access to different orders of meaning, the restricted code to *particularistic* meanings rooted in the here and now, in which principles are never made explicit and therefore not made available to inspection and change; the elaborated code, by contrast, to *universalistic* meanings which make principles and operations explicit and thus give individuals access to the grounds of their experience – grounds which, therefore, they can change. Unlike the restricted code, the elaborated code makes possible 'the liberation of speech from its evoking structure and it can take on an autonomy'.

(d) The concepts, *universalistic* and *particularistic*, are linked to two others, *context-free and context-bound*. The speaker of the restricted code is tied to the immediate situation, with the result that his speech can be understood only by the participants. On the other hand, the elaborated code, freed from this limitation, makes meaning available to all.

(e) The restricted code operates through *metaphor* and condensed symbols; whereas in the elaborated code, condensed symbol gives way to rationality.

All these differences are connected with a family typology so that we find the restricted code in the *positional* working class family, and the elaborated code in the middle class *personal* family.* The former has a clear-cut authority structure and its members are treated according to their status; the latter is based on genuine differences between persons with their unique attributes.

*The family typology is much more complicated than this, but no evidence is offered for it. See Bernstein, 1971, p. 152.

C

The Concept of Class in Bernstein

Bernstein concludes a recent paper, in which most of the ideas I have just peremptorily summarized are expounded, with these words:

> I have tried to show how the class system acts upon the deep structure of communication in the process of socialization. (Bernstein, 1971, p. 187)

Whatever else he has done, he has not done that – for the simple reason that he never examines the class system. By implication only, we are provided with a system consisting of two classes, called the working class and the middle class. The working class in his discussion are for the most part the unskilled working class. No further attempt is made at differentiation, whether in terms of history, traditions, job experience, ethnic origins, residential patterns, level of organization or class consciousness.* As a sociologist, Bernstein is content with the popular term 'middle class' to cover the varied strata whose relationship to the class system varies widely and whose class position certainly has important and different influences on their language. Hence the difference between the language of professors of sociology and that of minor civil servants. But, strangest of all in this system, the ruling class do not figure at all. When Bernstein talks of social control he is not talking of the ways in which one class controls or is controlled by another, but only of the ways in which members of the same class control each other.

Much of the language which the working class encounter

---

*In Brandis and Henderson, 1970, there is a complex statistical discussion (p. 130) of how an 'index of social class' was worked out for some of Bernstein's research. The statement of 'the problem' at the outset is limited entirely to 'occupational status' and 'educational status'. There is no discussion of the class system.

in their daily lives is transmitted to them through a variety of agencies not under their control which deploy a language designed to mystify, to intimidate and to create a sense that the present arrangement of society is immutable. Certain strata of the bureaucracy acquire this language as a vital part of their formation. There is nothing universalistic or person-oriented about it. Nobody knows exactly what part their family upbringing and education play in the acquisition of this highly marketable commodity.

A thorough attempt to analyse the relationship between class and language would require us to examine the relationship of the dominant culture of our society to the culture of the dominated. This would inevitably involve an examination of the part played by language in the operation of this relationship. No one, so far as I know, has attempted to do this. I believe that one thing which would emerge from such an undertaking would be that the linguistic capital of the dominant culture is persistently overvalued and that of the dominated culture persistently undervalued.

What effect does Bernstein's approach to class have on his analysis? He is aware that to describe certain characteristics of working class speech explains nothing. His explanation lies in the socializing agencies which are listed as family, school, peer group and work. Before we look more closely at that, we should notice two things about this picture of socialization, namely that it omits two powerful agencies of socialization. First, the media of communication, which, though they are largely in the hands of the ruling class, also have included since the beginning of the nineteenth century the published writings, pamphleteering, propaganda and theorizing of the working class. Second, and much more important, the organizations created by and maintained by the working class themselves. I mean everything from political parties, trade unions and non-conformist chapels to brass bands and pigeon-racing clubs.

To return to the socializing agencies, it is a feature of the analysis that they remain a list, and that no attempt is made to attribute to any one a key role. However, no reader could be blamed for assuming that key role to be played by the family, since no effort is made to examine the others. All attention is directed towards the home. No attention is paid to that vast area of critical working class experience, the encounter with exploitation at the place of work and the response to it; nor to the ways which take workers beyond the 'particularistic' circumstances of day-to-day work experience and move them on to explore the theory and practice of how to change society. Thus the working class child, marooned in the family with his authoritarian father and status-oriented mother, appears by omission to be denied for ever access to an elaborated code and its benefits, since he is alienated from the only agency which could give it to him, school.

It would not be true to say that Bernstein pays no attention at all to work experience and how it relates to his theory. He devotes one highly significant paragraph to it:

If a social group by virtue of its class relation, that is as a result of its common occupational function and social status, has developed strong communal bonds; if the work relation of this group offers little variety or little exercise in decision-making; if assertion, if it is to be successful, must be a collective rather than an individual act; if the work task requires physical manipulation and control rather than symbolic organisation and control; if the diminished authority of the man at work is transformed into an authority of power at home; if the home is over-crowded and limits the variety of situations it can offer; if the children socialize each other in an environment offering little intellectual stimuli; if all these attributes are found in one setting, then it is plausible to assume that such a social setting will generate a particular form of communication which will shape the intellectual, social and affective orientation of the children. (Bernstein, 1971, p. 143)

This telling passage gives us no indication of the source of the information and understanding offered to us. Or to put it more bluntly, how does the writer know about these features of working class life? Do his ideas derive from a study of workers in industry? Which industry? Where? Or are we being offered a stereotype of the unskilled worker assembled from the descriptive literature of sociology? We are given seven and a half conditions for the existence of the restricted code – and notice that *all* must be present before the 'plausible assumption' about communication can be made. Are we to assume that they are all of equal importance? If they are, we are entitled to assume that they will become criteria for Bernstein's subsequent assertions and in the research that he cites. They are certainly not criteria for his research samples (see footnote on p. 66), and some of the criteria are never mentioned again, while others are simply asserted in other forms. Let us look at them more closely.

Common occupational function and social status: I assume that what Bernstein means is that all workers have to sell their labour power, and that the ones he is talking about have to do so relatively cheaply – though he does not say so. However, this primary characteristic conceals the fact that different sections of the working class differ in very important secondary characteristics which in turn will affect how they use language. These characteristics should make us hesitate before we accept the invitation to join in the 'plausible assumption'. This is no simple matter of dividing the working class into 'skilled' and 'unskilled', nor of the niceties of the Halls-Jones scale.* We must distinguish between those who are quiescent and defeated and

---

*The classification of workers into 'skilled' and 'unskilled' seems to bear little relation to the level of skill required in their jobs, and to have more to do with their power to win that grading from their employers. Agricultural labourers would be a case in point.

those who are articulate, highly verbal, between those who are submerged in what Freire (1971) calls 'the culture of silence' and others who are capable of being quite explicit about principles and operations in those areas of experience which have been their universities. As the American sociologist, Labov, has pointed out, our knowledge of the relationship of language and work is based on 'meager anecdotal evidence or on lexical lists which have little social significance' (Labov, 1971).

What distinguishes the language of Liverpool dockers from that of Durham miners or Clydeside shipbuilders or London railwaymen or Coventry car workers? Or for that matter, what distinguishes the language of Liverpool dockers from that of London dockers? If questions of this kind are not asked, then we take away from people their history, be they working class or middle class. Though we have nobody who has done the kind of work in language that Hobsbawm (1964) and Thompson (1963) have done in history, we have no right to assume a linguistic uniformity based on general 'occupational function and status'. Indeed in their pages we can hear snatches of working class language which might prove to be a guide. A History Workshop publication like Douglass's *Pit Life in Co. Durham* (1972) shows just how much there is to be learnt. In the absence of any serious study, I would suggest that the most articulate workers are those who have actively participated in the creation and maintenance of their own organizations, and amongst those the most articulate would be those who in that process had encountered and helped to formulate theories about society and how to change it. (There is a political geography to that. It is more likely to happen in Fife than in Cheltenham.) There are other strands which need teasing out, like the tradition of certain kinds of nonconformity and the persistence of an oral tradition among Irish workers. It takes a Ewan

MacColl or Charles Parker to have an ear for such things. (See, for example, Parker, 1972.)

Little exercise in decision making: This essentially is an outsider's view, and the studies of the History Workshop on job control show just how little the outsider knows about such matters. In addition, of course, as I have suggested, there are areas of decision which are not directly related to the actual performance of the job.

Assertion is a collective rather than an individual act: Since this theme runs right through Bernstein's thesis, it is worth dwelling on. I am not sure what exactly is meant by 'assertion'. Utterances through a spokesman, or asserting themselves in other ways – collective bargaining, demonstrations, strikes and so on? But in either case this notion is totally untenable and even pernicious. What this kind of formulation does, especially for certain kinds of reader, is to conflate the concept of solidarity with mindless conformity and a sheep-like response to undercurrents in the herd. It implies that since the outcome of the experience of a group is the decision to act together, it has not been preceded either by what Bernstein calls 'the exploration of individual differences' or, we can add, by prolonged formal and informal debate about alternative courses of action. These activities can occur only if language is available which is adequate to the task. What kind of people imagine that the 1972 miners' strike, for example, was made possible merely by the incantation of a few rabble-rousing slogans?

The home and the peer group: I lump these together because there is already enough work in the United States to show that the assertions which have been made repeatedly about working class family life and the peer group have very little substance. I have in mind work such as Ginsburg's *The Myth of the Deprived Child* (1972), Ryan's *Blame the Victim* (1971), and Labov's work which I shall turn to shortly. Above all they show how the assertions are rarely based on observation of life as it is lived, much less on participation in it. Bernstein's own research suffers from a similar limitation.

The general drift of what I have had to say so far is that the relationship of the theory to the texture of reality is at best tenuous. There are some occasions when the argument does attempt to bring the two closer together, but in a particular way that I want to examine; at the same time this will provide the opportunity to say a little about the elaborated code and the middle class.

Imagine a husband and wife have just come out of the cinema, and are talking about the film: 'What do you think?' 'It had a lot to say.' 'Yes, I thought so too – let's go to the Millers, there may be something going on there.' They arrive at the Millers, who ask about the film. An hour is spent in the complex, moral, political, aesthetic subtleties of the film and its place in the contemporary scene. Here we have an elaborated variant; the meanings now have to be made public to others who have not seen the film. The speech shows careful editing, at both the grammatical and lexical levels. It is no longer context-tied. The meanings are explicit, elaborated and individualized. Whilst expressive channels are clearly relevant, the burden of meaning inheres predominantly in the verbal channel. The experience of the listeners cannot be taken for granted. Thus each member of the group is on his own as he offers his interpretation. Elaborated variants of this kind involve the speakers in particular role relationships, and if you cannot manage the role, you can't produce the appropriate speech. For as the speaker proceeds to individualize his meanings, he is differentiated from others like a figure from its ground. (Bernstein, 1971, p. 177)

This is strange indeed. We are presented with a hypothetical case in which the *content* of a conversation is summarized. That non-existent conversation is then commented on as though the actual text were in front of us ('The speech shows careful editing', etc.). We are in no position to agree or disagree. After a decade of research we are entitled to expect something better than this for our scrutiny, something which would permit alternative explanations. Let us, however, accept the example at its face value and write the missing paragraphs from the fiction for ourselves. It then becomes impossible to take it seriously as a contribution to the argument. For after all we have here Hampstead Man, not Orpington Man, and remember the elaborated code is supposed to be characteristic of the whole middle class. It is only when we return to the explanation of universalistic meanings and the high-level intellectualism it implies that we appreciate the reasons for the example. But we are given no reason for believing that this kind of discussion is diffused throughout the various strata of the middle class. Now it is quite true that earlier in the same paper (p. 175) we are told that only 'a tiny handful are given access to the principles of intellectual change', but we are not told who they are. Yet if this is true, then the whole of the argument about educability can be dismissed, for no explanation would be left of why middle class children *in general* succeed in school.

Of course, sections of the middle class differ from the working class in *what* they talk about and in their linguistic style. It is also true that many occupy posts in which their capacity to manipulate language in certain ways is what they sell to their employers. Consider all those working in clerical-administrative posts who in their working lives do no more than re-shuffle prefabricated verbal formulae or are the transmitters of the messages of others from above to below. Nothing universalistic about that. Certain sections of the middle class are intensely aware of language but in a particular way: they are concerned to express not so much difference from other individuals but conformity; the differences to which they give the closest attention are those verbal tokens which separate them from the working class. Hence the unwavering vigilance they maintain over the language of their children, guarding them even against such threats as 'grammar school cockney'. As Bourdieu puts it:

The 'realism of the structure' which is inherent in such a sociology of language [i.e. Bernstein's] tends to exclude from the field of research the social conditions from which that system of attitudes arises which orders, among other things, the structure of language. To take only one example, the distinctive traits of middle-class language such as hyper-correction of errors and the proliferation of signs of grammatical control are indices – among others – of a language characterised by anxious reference to norms legitimised by academic correction – for example, the concern for good manners, manners at the table or manners of speech which betray the language habits of the petit bourgeois. This sort of worry is expressed even more clearly by the avid search to acquire techniques of social behaviour shown by aspiring classes in manuals of etiquette or guides to the proper usage of language. One can see that this relationship to language is the integrating part of a system of attitudes to culture which rests upon the simple desire to respect a cultural rule which is recognised rather than understood, and upon the rigorous attention paid to the rule. This desire in the last analysis expresses the objective characteristics of the condition and position of the middle strata of the class structure. (Bourdieu and Passeron, 1970, p. 146, H.R.'s translation)

This does not mean that many middle class speakers do not use some, but not all, of the resources of language more freely and confidently than many, but not all, working class speakers. *How* they use those resources is another matter – and it cannot be automatically elevated by calling it 'universalistic'.

Enough of the Millers and their friends. After discussing them, the same text leaps to five-year-olds in order to demonstrate the difference between context-bound and context-free. Here is the passage:

Consider the two following stories which Peter Hawkins, Assistant Research Officer in the Sociological Research Unit, University of London Institute of Education, constructed as a result of his analysis of the speech of middle-class and working-class five-year-old children. The children were given a series of four pictures which told a story and they were invited to tell the story.

Here are the stories:

(1) Three boys are playing football and one boy kicks the ball and it goes through the window the ball breaks the window and the boys are looking at it and a man comes out and shouts at them because they've broken the window so they run away and then that lady looks out of her window and she tells the boys off.

(2) They're playing football and he kicks it and it goes through there it breaks the window and they're looking at it and he comes out and shouts at them because they've broken it so they run away and then she looks out and she tells them off.

With the first story the reader does not have to have the four pictures which were used as the basis for the story, whereas in the case of the second story the reader would require the initial pictures in order to make sense of the story. (Bernstein, 1971, p. 178)

You will notice these are *not* stories told by actual children, but are constructed by Hawkins who, in his own research report, calls them 'slightly exaggerated' (Hawkins, 1969), and who nevertheless had several hundreds of the original stories to choose from. Once again, let us take them at their face value – archetypes, if you will. The middle class child tells his story in a way that enables us to follow it without the pictures, the working class child does not. In grammatical terms the middle class child uses a more differentiated noun phrase. Thus, we are told, he generates universalistic meanings. So this is what those giants have dwindled to. If there is a route from these bare little stories, elicited on demand and not from a genuine wish to tell anyone a real story, to the Millers' universalistic flights, then we are given no description of it. There is a vast lacuna to be filled in. And there is another interesting point here. The argument runs that the working class child takes up a communalized role as against an individualized one. Yet in this instance, bearing in mind that the researcher and the child are both looking at the same set of pictures, it is clear that it is the working class child who is responding to the person. What needs to be explained is why the middle class child ignores him. Now it seems that in another experiment the children were left much more free in their construction of stories (they were invited to tell stories about dolls), and in this instance the working class children's stories were 'freer, longer, more imaginative', while those of the middle class children were 'dominated by the form of the narrative' (p. 180). The route to universalistic meanings cannot be through attention to form rather than content.

I have tried to make the following criticisms of Bernstein's work:

(1) It is based on an inadequate concept of class which lacks theoretical support.

(2) Arising from that, he presents a stereotyped view of working class life in general and its language in particular.

(3) Further, he attributes to middle class speakers in general certain rare and remarkable intellectual virtues, but there is an inadequate examination of the way in which their language is affected by their class position.

Educability

My own interest in this matter relates to educability. On this subject there is an ambiguity in Bernstein's stance, or at least a tension between some of his ideas and others. Without any question there can be found throughout his work a persistent concern that education should be re-shaped to accommodate the working class child by em-bodying *his* values and *his* culture. It is probably this fact more than any other which has made the rest of his work acceptable to so many educational progressives, though no doubt some are dazzled by the terminology which has a radical and even Marxist flavour.* This concern is tied to giving working class children access to the elaborated code, a concept which is explained in such a way that it furnishes no guide to possible strategies and can be made to justify quite contradictory practices.

Commentators frequently draw attention to the fact that the restricted code is never denigrated by Bernstein, but that on the contrary he holds it up for admiration and respect. There is indeed an almost obligatory paragraph which appears in the papers. Here it is:

One of the difficulties of the approach is to avoid implicit value judgments about the relative worth of speech systems and the cultures which they symbolize. Let it be said immediately that a restricted code gives access to a vast potential of meanings, of delicacy, subtlety and diversity of cultural forms, to a unique aesthetic the basis of which in condensed symbols may influence the form of the imagining. Yet, in complex industrialized societies its differently focused experience may be disvalued and humiliated within schools, or seen, at best, to be irrelevant to the educational endeavour. For the schools are predicated upon elaborated code and its system of social relationships. Although an elaborated code does not entail any specific value system, the value system of the middle class penetrates the texture of the very learning context itself. (Bernstein, 1971, p. 186)

It must be acknowledged without reserve that these remarks constitute a powerful recognition of the poten-tialities of working class speech. At the same time it must

* In the most recent papers, Marx is cited by Bernstein as a forma-tive influence.

be said that remarks of this sort are always essentially *parenthetic*, in the sense that they are never explored and they are made in a context which explores tirelessly and intricately what the restricted code cannot do. What is this 'vast potential of meanings', and why have they not been subject to the same intensive investigation and research as the other ideas in the theory? Elsewhere, some of us have argued (Barnes, Britton and Rosen, 1971) that expressive language is persistently outlawed in schools, especially in those areas of the curriculum which supposedly demand the elaborated code – history, science, etc. – in which school pupils are obliged to undergo a strange linguistic apprenticeship. In any case, the respect accorded to the restricted code has a hollow ring when 'rationality' is excluded from it ('restricted codes draw upon metaphor, whereas elaborated codes draw upon rationality'). How can this be free from value judgements? As Blackburn has pointed out:

Once theories are thoroughly cleansed of all 'value judgements' it is believed that they will be governed only by the wholesome discipline of objective facts. The predictable consequence of this attempted purge of values is to orient theory and research towards certain crude, over-abstracted value notions masquerading as scientific concepts: e.g. 'utility', 'efficiency', 'productivity', 'equilibrium', 'rationality', etc. (Blackburn, 1969)

It cannot be repeated too often that, for all Bernstein's work, we know little about working class language. For me the parenthesis is more important than the rest of the text.

There is one Bernstein paper which more than any other is seen by educational progressives as a successful answer to criticisms and, significantly, it is a paper to be found in left wing company, the reply to the Black Papers, *Education for Democracy* (Rubinstein and Stoneman, 1970). This paper shows all the signs of being an attempt by Bernstein to align himself unambiguously in educational politics. In his stated attitudes he most certainly does so; but the attempt to fit these attitudes to the theory is less convincing, for as the Jewish proverb has it, he is trying to dance at two weddings at the same time.

The paper begins with an attack on the concept of compensatory education, for directing attention away from the inadequacies of the schools to the inadequacies of families:

> The concept of 'compensatory education' serves to direct attention away from the internal organization and the educational context of the school, and focus our attention upon the families and children. The concept 'compensatory education' implies that something is lacking in the family, and so in the child. As a result the children are unable to benefit from schools. It follows then that the school has to 'compensate' for the something which is missing in the family and the children become little deficit systems. If only the parents were interested in the goodies we offer; if only they were like middle-class parents, then we could do our job. Once the problem is seen even implicitly in this way, then it becomes appropriate to coin the terms 'cultural deprivation', 'linguistic deprivation' etc. And then these labels do their own sad work. (Bernstein, 1971, p. 192)

Anyone who takes the trouble to read from end to end the papers written over the last decade will find that what Bernstein is criticizing is almost an exact description of his own work. Time and time again we are given an analysis of the positional and personal families, the family is said to be the microcosm of the social macrocosm, mothers are asked questions about how they would speak to their children, answer their questions, etc. As we have seen, Bernstein's theory, too, has it that there is 'something lacking' in working class language: it is called elaborated code and the very same paper goes on to say so. You cannot protest very convincingly against the harm done by the label, 'linguistic deprivation', when your own theory points to a

deficit, indeed when you have actually stated elsewhere that
'the normal linguistic environment of the working class is
one of relative deprivation' (Bernstein, 1971, p. 66) and
that the codes 'are highly resistant to change' (op. cit.,
p. 91). The labels 'restricted' and 'elaborated' also 'do
their own sad work'. It is true that this paper puts most
trenchantly the dilemma of the working class child in the
middle class school, but it did not require the codes theory
to do any of this.

Anyone looking for a published scholarly viewpoint
which is the opposite to Bernstein's should study William
Labov's powerful and committed account of black working
class language. You will look in vain in this country for a
similar socio-linguistic account of Cockney, Geordie or
other working class dialects. It is impossible to do justice
to it here. But I must attempt some indication. Labov sets
out to show that the concept of verbal deprivation has no
basis in social reality –

. . . in fact, Negro children in the urban ghettos receive a great
deal of verbal stimulation, hear more well-formed sentences than
middle-class children, and participate fully in a highly verbal
culture. They have the same basic vocabulary, possess the same
capacity for conceptual learning, and use the same logic as
anyone else who learns to speak and understand English.

The notion of verbal deprivation is part of the modern
mythology of educational psychology, typical of the unfounded
notions which tend to expand rapidly in our educational system.
In past decades linguists have been as guilty as others in promoting such intellectual fashions at the expense of both teachers
and children. But the myth of verbal deprivation is particularly
dangerous, because it diverts attention from real defects of our
educational system to imaginary defects of the child. (Labov,
1972, p. 179)

Labov studies the language of those totally alienated
from the school who 'participate fully in the vernacular

culture of the street'. He shows in quite precise terms, examining stretches of *recorded* conversation, how the usual research situation reduces working class language almost to zero, and how by changing that situation, by allowing a hitherto 'non-verbal' child to bring a friend, by introducing a taboo topic and by having the interviewer sit on the floor, etc., the same child becomes highly articulate – because, he argues, the culture from which he comes is a highly verbal one. He then turns his attention to middle class speech:

There are undoubtedly many verbal skills which children from ghetto areas must learn in order to do well in the school situation, and some of these are indeed characteristic of middle-class verbal behaviour. Precision in spelling, practice in handling abstract symbols, the ability to state explicitly the meaning of words and a richer knowledge of the Latinate vocabulary, may all be useful acquisitions. But is it true that *all* of the middle class verbal habits are functional and desirable in the school situation?/ Before we impose middle class verbal style upon children from other cultural groups, we should find out how much of this is useful for the main work of analyzing and generalizing, and how much is merely stylistic / or even dysfunctional. In high school and college, middle class children spontaneously complicate their syntax to the point that instructors despair of getting them to make their language simpler and clearer. In every learned journal one can find examples of jargon and empty elaboration – and complaints about it./ Is the 'elaborated code' of Bernstein really so 'flexible, detailed and subtle' as some psychologists believe? (Jensen, 1968, p. 119) Isn't it also turgid, redundant, and empty? Is it not simply an elaborated *style*, rather than a superior code or system?/ (Labov, 1972, p. 192)

Labov supports this with a detailed analysis of two texts, one from Larry, a fifteen-year-old, the roughest and loudest member of a Harlem gang on the subject of belief in Heaven and Hell; and the other from Charles M, an upper middle class, college educated Negro, on the subject of witchcraft. He comes to the conclusion that Larry is undoubtedly a skilled speaker with verbal presence of mind, who can use the English language for many purposes; but that Charles M is merely an educated speaker.

> The initial impression of him as a good speaker is simply our long-conditioned reaction to middle class verbosity. We know that people who use these stylistic devices are educated people, and we are inclined to credit them with saying something intelligent. Our reactions are accurate in one sense. Charles M is more educated than Larry. But is he more rational, more logical, more intelligent? Is he any better at thinking out a problem to its solution? Does he deal more easily with abstractions? There is no reason to think so. Charles M succeeds in letting us know that he is educated, but in the end we do not know what he is trying to say, and neither does he. (ibid., p. 169)

Labov also poses a problem which he says nobody has yet tackled:

> When Bernstein (e.g. 1966) describes his elaborated code in general terms, it emerges as a subtle and sophisticated mode of planning utterances, where the speaker is achieving structural variety, taking the other person's knowledge into account, and so on. But when it comes to describing the actual difference between middle class and working class speakers (Bernstein 1966) we are presented with a proliferation of 'think', of the passive, of modals and auxiliaries, of the first-person pronoun, of uncommon words, and so on. But these are the bench marks of hemming and hawing, backing and filling, that are used by Charles M, the devices which so often obscure whatever positive contribution education can make to our use of language. When we have discovered how much of middle class style is a matter of fashion and how much actually helps us express ideas clearly, we will have done ourselves a great service. We will then be in a position to say what standard grammatical rules must be taught to nonstandard speakers in the early grades. (ibid., p. 171)

Labov enters the linguistic deprivation battle boldly selecting his targets (Jensen, Engleman and Bereiter, et al.) and produces the detailed linguistic analysis to support his argument. Why is there no English Labov?

A final point on educability. We are informed repeatedly by Bernstein that 'schools are predicated upon the elaborated code' (Bernstein, 1971, p. 186). No attempt is made, in fact, to examine how language is really used in schools most of the time. Some of us who have been studying tapes of language in school would say that very frequently, especially in the secondary system, there is an actual *reduction* in the range of pupils' language in many school lessons. There are many other things one would want to say about the way in which language is used and unused in school, but one thing is certain – Bernstein's alluring descriptions of the elaborated code do not fit it.

What evidence is presented for the validity of Bernstein's theories? Over the last two years some five volumes (Brandis and Henderson, 1970; Gahagan and Gahagan, 1970; Turner and Mohan, 1970; Robinson and Rackshaw, 2 vols, 1972) have appeared in rapid succession, and more are promised. I cannot at this stage do more than make some general comments on this work. Before I do so, let me stress that I am not concerned to examine details of research methodology or, with hindsight, to tut-tut over the limitations of what was or was not discovered. I would readily agree that any investigator would have been bound to stumble and grope in the thickets of design and execution.

The theory, remember, claims to be a vast overarching structure, linking the class structure of society to language, socialization, cultural transmission and cognitive development. The evidence of the research is based on studies of the family and young children. We must further limit this by adding that the mother's language is represented not by

what she says and does, but by what she says she would say
or do. And the child, not by observation of the free flow
of his language, but in the 'laboratory' situation. The
hazards of this kind of work are well known. As we have
seen, Labov has shown the part played by eliciting techniques in giving a totally false picture of working class
language.

Thus, at its best, the research can shed light on only one
small area of the vast territory covered by the theory. In
that small area we discover, sometimes in grammatical
terms, sometimes in semantic terms, that there are differences between working class speech and middle class
speech and these are interpreted in terms of the theory.
They do not strengthen it. For example, if a middle class
child uses more expressions signifying uncertainty it does
not necessarily mean that he is able to tolerate the state of
uncertainty any more than the child who does not.

I tried to indicate earlier that sensitive awareness of
working class life and middle class life would direct our
enquiries elsewhere. To acquire this awareness we would
need the active, informed help of the very people whose
language is being studied, and this presupposes a very
different approach to research altogether.

Conclusion

In all that I have said I may possibly have given the impression that I believe that working class speech is as fine
an instrument as could be devised for communication and
thinking, and that middle class speech is pretentious verbiage. That would be absurd romanticism. I *am* saying that
the relationship between class and speech cannot be described or understood by the usual sociological methods.
Working class speech has its own strengths which the
normal linguistic terminology has not been able to catch.

There is no sharp dividing line between it and any other kind of speech, but infinite variations in the deployment of the resources of language. I do think there are aspects of language usually acquired through education which, given favourable circumstances, give access to more powerful ways of thinking; but given the conditions of life of many strata of the middle class, the language acquired through education can conceal deserts of ignorance. Moreover, the middle class have often to pay a price for the acquisition of certain kinds of transactional language, and that is loss of vitality and expressiveness, and obsession with proprieties.

Those are very vague alternatives to the theoretical elegances which I have criticized, and this points to a profound weakness in all I have said. I have at several points noted that we do not know much about the relationship between language and class. It is time to find out.

References

Bantock, G. H., *Education and Social Values*, Faber and Faber 1965

Barnes, D., Britton, J., and Rosen, H., *Language, the Learner and the School* (revised edition), Penguin 1971

Bernstein, B., *Class, Codes and Control*, Vol. 1, Routledge and Kegan Paul 1971

Blackburn, R., 'A Brief Guide to Bourgeois Ideology', in A. Cockburn and R. Blackburn (eds), *Student Power*, Penguin 1969

Bourdieu, P., and Passeron, J., *La réproduction*, Editions Minuit 1970

Brandis, W., and Henderson, D., *Social Class, Language and Communication*, Routledge and Kegan Paul 1970

Cazden, C. B., 'The Neglected Situations in Child Language', in F. Williams (ed.), *Language and Poverty*, Markham 1970

Douglass, D., *Pit Life in Co. Durham*, History Workshop Pamphlet No. 6, Ruskin College, Oxford, 1972

Freire, P., *Pedagogy of the Oppressed*, Herder and Herder 1971

Gahagan, D. M., and Gahagan, G. A., *Talk Reform*, Routledge and Kegan Paul 1970

Ginsburg, H., *The Myth of the Deprived Child*, Prentice-Hall 1972

Hawkins, P. R., 'Social Class, the Nominal Group and Reference', in *Language and Speech*, 12, 2, 1969

Henry, J., *Essays in Education*, Penguin 1971

Hobsbawm, E., *Labouring Men*, Weidenfeld and Nicolson 1964

Jackson, B., *Working-class Community*, Penguin 1968

Jensen, A. R., 'Social Class and Verbal Learning', in Deutch, Katz and Jensen (eds), *Social Class, Race and Psychological Development*, Holt, Reinhart and Winston 1968

Labov, W., 'Variation in Language', in C. Reed (ed.), *The Learning of Language*, Appleton-Century-Crofts 1971

Labov, W., 'The Logic of Non-standard English', in P. Giglioli (ed.), *Language and Social Context*, Penguin 1972

Parker, C., 'Towards a People's Culture', *Tract*, No. 3, The Gryphon Press, Brechfa, Llanon, Cardiganshire, 1972

Robinson, W. P., and Rackshaw, S. J., *A Question of Answers*, Routledge and Kegan Paul 1972

Rubinstein, D., and Stoneman, C., *Education for Democracy*, Penguin 1970

Ryan, W., *Blaming the Victim*, Pantheon 1971

Simon, B., *Intelligence Testing and the Comprehensive School*, Lawrence and Wishart 1953

Thompson, E., *The Making of the English Working Class*, Penguin 1963

Turner, G. J., and Mohan, B. A., *A Linguistic Description and Computer Program for Children's Speech*, Routledge and Kegan Paul 1970

Vernon, P., *Secondary School Selection*, Methuen 1957

Vernon, P., *Intelligence and Attainment Tests*, ULP 1960

Reading Guide

A good starting-point would be *Language and Poverty* edited by F. Williams (Markham, 1970). This presents differing and opposings points of view but does enable most of the important issues to emerge.

An attempt to relate socio-linguistic theory to the education of working-class children can be found in *Functions of Language in the Classroom* edited by C. Cazden, V. John and D. Hughes (Teachers' College, Columbia University, 1972).

Both the above collections contain pieces by Bernstein and those who wish to trace the development and modification of his views will find them best represented in *Class, Codes and Control*, Vol. 1, by B. Bernstein (Routledge and Kegan Paul 1971).

For basic theory about the relationship between language and thinking the best starting-point is *Thought and Language* by L. S. Vigotsky (MIT Press). How this relationship has been explored in research is well represented in *Language* edited by R. C. Oldfield and J. C. Marshall (Penguin) and *Language in Thinking* edited by P. Adams (Penguin).

Readers will find that the literature on 'deprivation' is predominately American, particularly those works which are challenging the theories which dominated the sixties. The same is true of powerful descriptive books written by teachers of the 'disadvantaged', like *36 Children* by H. Kohl (Penguin) and *Death at an Early Age* by Kozl (Penguin).

A remarkable venture is *Centreprise* (66 Dalston Lane, Hackney, London) which is producing material including poems, stories and autobiographical accounts of the people of Hackney. *Oral History*, 'an occasional news sheet' (distributed by Paul Thompson, Department of Sociology, University of Essex), is full of valuable material.

As a result of the paper which constitutes this chapter a small group was formed which has produced *Language and Class Workshop 1* (February 1974): others are to follow.

4. The Politics of Culture

Graham Murdock

Introduction

It isn't only the language of working class people that is persistently misrepresented by educationists. Their whole value-system is similarly misunderstood and the conflict between this and the dominant values treated in terms of simple rejection. Graham Murdock shows that the idea of culture is usually vastly over-simplified and takes no account of alternative meanings which may be held by the working class and those who have sought, from the beginning, to use state schools as an instrument of domination. He traces various strands of opposition to the dominant idea-system.

Graham Murdock studied sociology at the London School of Economics and at the University of Sussex. Since 1968 he has been a member of the Centre for Mass Communication Research where one of his main interests has been in exploring the relationships between education and the mass media.

Tom Jones by Henry Fielding, Jane Austen's *Pride and Prejudice*, Charlotte Bronte's *Jane Eyre* . . . the Literary Heritage Collection volumes contain the immortal masterpieces that every cultured person intends to read . . . Printed on fine quality paper with elegant typography, they form a lifetime collection proclaiming your good taste as a decorator and your discernment as a reader . . . Your friends will admire the sumptuous period bindings and perhaps even envy you for owning them.

This blurb, which is taken from a glossy advertisement for a book club, illustrates several important things about the way the word 'culture' is usually used.

The world of 'culture' presented in this advertisement is a world of objects; pictures to hang on the wall, books to furnish a room. More particularly, it is a world made up of the 'masterpieces' produced by exceptionally gifted individuals. By definition then, most people can only consume 'culture', they cannot produce it. Being cultured is therefore a matter of collecting the appropriate cultural objects and experiences, and being able to talk about them in the correct terms. Being cultured is in turn presented as a mark of superior intellect and discernment, an indication that the person is a distinct cut above the average, someone to look up to, to 'admire and perhaps even envy'. According to this widely publicized definition then, culture consists of the things produced by artists and intellectuals for cultivated audiences. It is no accident, for example, that works of culture are usually housed in special buildings set aside for the purpose – museums, art galleries, and theatres. It symbolizes the fact that culture is seen as something out of the ordinary, something removed from most people's everyday lives.

'Politics', on the other hand, is very definitely presented as being about the basic facts of daily life, such as prices, jobs and housing. More specifically, politics is identified with the ways these bread and butter issues are defined and dealt with by the main parliamentary parties. Politicians do of course have policies for the arts, and some public money is spent on supporting cultural institutions and activities, but by and large politics is supposed to be kept out of culture.

Clearly then, before I can discuss the 'politics of culture' I must begin by providing alternative definitions of these terms. This is not simply a matter of academic hair splitting.

Acceptance of available definitions necessarily entails a tacit support for the social order which they describe. Consequently, any challenge to the existing situation requires a challenge to the language which endorses it. Opening up alternative ways of describing and thinking about the present is a necessary step in formulating the possibilities for the future.

By culture, I mean firstly the pattern of ideas, beliefs and values through which people make sense of their experiences, and secondly, the various means through which they communicate this sense of themselves and their situation. This stress on communication is crucial because it highlights the central point that cultures are not primarily collections of objects, but stocks of shared understandings and responses accumulated in the course of confronting a common set of social conditions. They provide a pool of available meanings and modes of expression which people can draw upon to describe and respond to their own particular experiences. Far from being separated from everyday life therefore, involvement in culture is an integral part of people's continuing attempt to make sense of their situation and to find ways of coming to terms with it, or else of changing it.

Most complex societies contain a diversity of cultures corresponding roughly to the major social groupings. Contemporary Britain is no exception. This plurality is, however, more apparent than real. For although various cultures coexist, they do not all carry the same weight or exert the same influence; and it is at this point that politics becomes important.

We act politically whenever we attempt to make other people behave in ways that serve our own interests. The ability to get other people to do what we want, even if they themselves don't particularly want to, constitutes power. Politics in this sense, then, is not simply about what happens in Parliament or in the local town hall, but about the relations of domination and subordination and the balance between conformity and resistance in every sector of social life. The distribution of power tends to follow the distribution of wealth and property, which in Britain today is highly concentrated with the top ten per cent of the population owning nearly three-quarters of the personal wealth. Ownership and control over economic resources carries with it a considerable range of potential powers. The power to force up the price of land and houses, and the power to close down a factory and throw people out of work, provide obvious examples. Among the other equally important, but less obvious, powers accruing to economically dominant groups is their privileged access to, and control over, the major means of communication. Consequently, their particular ideas, values and modes of expression tend to receive insistent and pervasive publicity, and thus they come to permeate the consciousness of subordinate groups, and to provide at least some of the categories and standards through which they organize and evaluate their social experience. It is in this sense, then, that we can talk about the culture of dominant groups as the dominant culture.

Nevertheless, the unequal distribution of wealth and power tends to create problems for those in subordinate positions which the descriptions and explanations provided by the dominant culture cannot always paper over. Gaps appear between what is supposed to be going on and what is in fact happening; between what has been promised and what is actually being delivered. Faced with these gaps, those on the receiving end, who are predominantly working class, have developed their own cultures.

Historically, working class culture has been made up of a mixture of combative and accommodatory elements. The combative stream, represented primarily by the various radical strands of the Labour Movement, has consistently opposed the definitions provided by the dominant culture and demanded the redistribution of wealth and power. The accommodatory strand, on the other hand, has generally accepted the broad contours of the social order as more or less given, and has searched for ways of guaranteeing pleasure, diversion and security within the existing situation. The Co-operative Movement, the music halls and the working men's clubs provide instances of this accommodatory response. Despite the obvious and considerable differences between these two strands, they have a basic characteristic in common. They both represent attempts by ordinary people to contest the power of dominant groups and to establish some degree of control over the range and meaning of their social relationships and social experiences. They have both, therefore, developed through a continuing process of negotiation and struggle. In many cases, such as that of the trade union movement, this process has been open and often dramatic, involving the imprisonment of union officials and members; the physical intimidation of strikers, and the confiscation of union funds. In other instances, however, the struggle for control has taken more muted, less stark forms. The early history of working men's clubs provides a case in point.

The club movement began in earnest in 1862 when the celebrated temperance preacher, Henry Solly, backed by a consortium of aristocrats and industrialists, founded the Working Men's Club and Institute Union. From the beginning it was clear that the clubs represented attempts to contain and control the consciousness and activities of working men by encouraging them to participate in 'improving' recreational activities rather than involving themselves in political radicalism. The clubs were teetotal, but they provided entertainment facilities in order to attract an audience for their central activity: lectures propagating the assumptions and values of the dominant culture. As Solly candidly put it: 'recreation would provide a starting point for the "inclined plane" up which many of the working men and youths should be rolled into the lecture.' From the beginning, this definition of the nature and purpose of the clubs was contested by the rank and file membership. Drink was introduced in 1867, and in 1884 the rank and file gained a majority on the club movement's controlling council and voted to reject the financial support of their eminent patrons and to make the movement self-supporting out of members' contributions. From this point on, the clubs ceased to be organizations provided *for* working class people and became organizations controlled *by* them.

This instance is not particularly significant in itself, but it does illustrate the crucial point that the struggle by ordinary people to control the circumstances of their everyday lives takes place on two levels. It involves not only the struggle for control over material resources and institutional structures, but also the attempt to resist dominant definitions and to develop different ways of looking at the situation and its possibilities and alternative definitions of how facilities might be used and social relations organized. The politics of culture, then, is primarily about this struggle over contending definitions of what is possible, and historically schools have been a key site on which this struggle has taken place.

From its beginnings in the 1830s, the state sponsored school system was inextricably bound up with the business of social control, and more particularly with containing the radical, combative stream in working class culture. Sending working class children to school was seen not simply as a convenient way of instructing them in the basic skills required by a developing capitalist economy, but more importantly, as a way of familiarizing them with their future role as productive workers and compliant citizens and persuading them to work within this definition of the situation rather than against it. As Kay Shuttleworth, one of the leading Victorian educators, put it:

The great object to be kept in mind in regulating any school for the instruction of the children of the labouring class is the rearing of hardy, intelligent working men, whose character and habits shall afford the greatest amount of security to the property and order of the community . . . it is chiefly intended that the practical lesson, that they are destined to earn their livelihood by the sweat of their brow shall be inculcated.

This was written in 1838. But despite the considerable changes in the scope and structure of education which have occurred since then, schools continue to act as agencies of social control. They accomplish this by transmitting and reproducing both the dominant patterns of social class and power relations and the dominant culture which supports them.

There is abundant evidence to show that, by and large, the various sorting and assessment procedures employed in schools tend to operate against children from working class backgrounds and to consign them to the less prestigious and well-endowed sectors of the school system. As a result, comparatively few stay on much beyond the minimum leaving age, and most leave without amassing a significant stock of examination passes. However, as job chances and hence social class position are increasingly determined by the successful completion of a specified length and level of schooling as evidenced by the possession of the appropriate certificate, a vicious circle is established. By translating the social class position into educational advantage, and educational advantage back into class position, the schools perpetuate the existing pattern of economic advantage. The circle is not completely closed, however, and a certain proportion of working class pupils do manage, against the odds, to complete the educational race. But the success of this minority, far from denting the credibility of the system, lends it further support. In the first place it masks the operation of class inequalities and reinforces the dominant assumption that inherited privileges are a thing of the past and that in modern Britain social positions are allocated solely on the basis of individual ability and achievement. Secondly, it confirms the 'losers' in their submission by attributing their failure to their own personal inadequacies and deflecting attention away from the intrinsic unfairness of the competition itself.

The basic content of what is taught in schools is laid down in the curriculum. Traditionally the curriculum has been underpinned by a hierarchical classification of culture. Consequently, only certain sorts of knowledge and experience have been defined as suitable subjects for thinking and talking about in school, while others have been classified as unsuitable and have been excluded from consideration. The core of this classification process involves attaching the term culture exclusively to the ideas and forms of expression developed by, or on behalf of, dominant groups. In this way pupils have been given to understand that the finest and most valid forms of knowledge and expression are those developed by social and intellectual elites. Conversely, the cultural forms produced or enjoyed by subordinate groups have been classified as inferior and treated as non-negotiable currencies within the school system. Traditionally, therefore, the curriculum has enshrined the assumptions and forms of the dominant culture as the yardsticks against which other, contending, cultures have been measured and found wanting.

Consider these two quotations for example. The first one is taken from a recent book on English teaching by the

well-known educationalist and critic **David Holbrook**, and
the second one is from a handbook for music teachers.

I believe, it is time for conscience to speak a little more power-
fully. We can surely do so from our world of culture and sensibility. Let us compare the following 'pop' song with a genuine
poem. The song was sung by Mick Jagger with the usual
masturbatory gestures. (David Holbrook, *English in Australia
Now*, 1973)

The 'pop' disease is so widespread these days that no child
seems to escape it . . . To show disgust at the sounds of those
records (and they are undeniably disgusting) will achieve little.
Better to keep a calm face and insist on your pound of flesh. It is
after all a music period and not 'Housewives Choice'. . . .
(Terence Dwyer, *Teaching Musical Appreciation*, 1967)

The blank assertion of automatic and absolute superiority
contained in phrases such as 'our world of culture and
sensibility' and 'disgusting sounds' epitomize the cultural
elitism which still underpins a great deal of current educational thinking and practice.

Of course it is true that a lot of pop music is produced
simply to make money, and that much of it is trivial and
repetitious. But this is not the whole story. Pop music can
also be a means through which people can deepen their
awareness of themselves and their capacities, and extend
their understanding and insight into the experience of
others. In his book *This New Season*, Chris Searle describes how he discovered this when he began to read his
pupils' poems.

A fifteen-year-old boy takes a hit song, 'My Name is Jack', and
creates his own poem, achieving a deep empathy for one of the
social rejects of Spitalfields or Whitechapel . . . A school leaver
takes a sentimental song like 'Grandad', and recreates it as a
sympathetic insight into the experience of old age . . . Commercial pop music had turned to poetry: promoting sympathy and

mutual understanding, and strengthening both individual and collective identities.

The poems he reprints in the book bear him out. By refusing point blank to recognize this potentiality, David Holbrook and his supporters devalue the creative capacities of ordinary people, and dismiss out of hand the possibility that pupils may have something to offer teachers in the way of insight and understanding.

Of course, I have deliberately chosen rather blatant examples of cultural elitism in order to highlight my point. Many educationalists and teachers would be more guarded and cautious, and would probably prefer to use more scientific sounding language. The basic underlying assumptions, however, remain unchanged. It is only possible to have a concept like 'cultural deprivation' at all, for example, if you first have a firm definition of what counts as 'culture' and what doesn't.

The notion of 'culture' encapsulated in the curriculum and embodied in examination certificates plays a key role in supporting the existing social order. In contrast to the traditional elites who could claim that they were born to rule, the new meritocratic elites increasingly base their claim to power on the possession of the valued knowledge and expertise represented by educational certificates. They claim to be the ones 'in the know', the experts, whose training equips and entitles them to assume positions of management and control. Conversely, those who have not received this training and obtained the relevant certificates are encouraged to regard themselves as ignorant and incompetent and therefore only capable of occupying the subordinate positions to which they have been consigned.

The school's definition of what counts as valued knowledge and experience has not gone uncontested, however; indeed, it has often been a key focus of conflict between

D

the schools and their working class catchment areas. From the beginning of the modern system most working class people have seen schooling as a convenient way of acquiring knowledge and skills that would increase their bargaining power in the labour market, and have resisted the schools' attempts to impose the standards and expressive forms of the dominant culture. As one disgruntled father remarked in 1844, when a school inspector asked him what he wanted school to do for his children: 'We wants a bit of reading and writing and summing, but no'at else.'

In addition to underpinning the curriculum, the ideas and values of the dominant culture permeate the pattern of day-to-day activities and social relations within schools. Schools are, in fact, reproductions in miniature of the dominant social order and are governed by the same rules and assumptions: competitiveness, regulating activity by the clock, working hard and productively, and not arguing with or answering back to those in authority. Schools provide a dress rehearsal for adult working life. For the successful pupils this entails rehearsing the attributes and skills necessary for future career advancement – efficiency, loyalty, initiative, and the ability to deal with juniors and subordinates. For the remainder, it means rehearsing accommodations to a lifetime of following someone else's orders.

This account of conventional schooling is rather too static, however. Over the last few years the traditional structures I have described have been subjected to increasing criticisms and a number of organizational and curriculum innovations have been introduced. At first sight these developments seem to be opening up genuine alternatives. But on closer inspection much of the initial euphoria evaporates, and many of these innovations turn out to be the old structures reappearing under new labels or in slightly modified forms. A number of comprehensive schools, for example, are comprehensive in name only, either because the grammar schools in the area continue to cream off the ablest pupils, or else because the school operates its own internal sorting procedures which reproduce the essential features of the selective system under the same roof. A sleight of hand is also involved in a number of curriculum developments. Many of the most publicized innovations are responses to the raising of the school leaving age and the need to find ways of occupying the pupils who don't particularly want to stay on. Some of the solutions, such as the trend towards collaborative project work, do involve important departures from traditional ways of working. But, as long as these sorts of innovations are confined to the low status pupils, and as long as the more successful pupils continue with a curriculum geared to conventional examinations, the established hierarchical evaluations of knowledge and activity are left essentially unchallenged, and unchanged.

Tradition tends to cast a long shadow so that even when people appear to be creating something new they are apt to fall back on the familiar and to end up working within established frameworks. Genuine change, then, is not just a matter of modifying or even dismantling traditional structures; it is also a question of rejecting the dominant assumptions which underpin them, and evolving alternative definitions of what is possible. This does not mean that control over material resources is unimportant. On the contrary, if ideas are to be translated into concrete practice, it is ultimately decisive. Nevertheless, if change is to go beyond the reproduction or modification of what already exists, it must be informed by a thoroughgoing critique of what passes for education at the moment, and a clear alternative conception of what education could become.

Obviously this is a sizable task. But a start can be made

by challenging the dominant structures of education and the assumptions which support them.

At the present time, the school system makes a promise it cannot keep – the promise of equality of educational opportunity. The system only stipulates that everyone starts the educational obstacle race at the age of five; it does not guarantee that everyone will have the same chance of winning, or even of finishing the course. On the contrary, the rules of the race are quite explicitly rigged in favour of the children of parents who have already been successful competitors themselves. In order to redress this imbalance and to give every child a genuinely equal opportunity, in the sense of a real chance to develop whatever capacities they may have to the full, it is therefore essential to discriminate positively in favour of working class children. In other words, equality of opportunity can only be secured by a massive redistribution of educational resources. The Labour party have taken some basic steps in this direction with their proposals to extend the principle of Priority Areas and to make this a primary policy target. Given the insistent facts of income inequality and widespread urban poverty, it is absolutely essential that they are pressured to keep this promise. The redirection of resources is an essential precondition for equalizing opportunities, but as a further guarantee it is also necessary to continue to work towards the final dismantling of the selective system, and the establishment of genuinely comprehensive schools.

It would, however, be a great mistake to wait until these changes have been accomplished before challenging some of the other dominant definitions and practices. As Douglas Holly points out in his essay in this collection, change tends to work unevenly, and at the present time several innovations which potentially challenge dominant definitions and offer genuine alternatives are beginning to gather momentum.

What goes on in schools is primarily determined not by the needs and interests of the pupils and teachers, but by the demands of dominant groups, represented by the examination boards who set the syllabuses and by the pupils' future employers. Faced with this situation, it is scarcely surprising that many pupils come to see education not as a potential source of intrinsic interests and satisfaction but primarily as a commodity which can be cashed in for job chances. School for them is simply a means to an end. The pervasiveness of this instrumental attitude to school was graphically illustrated by the results of the Schools Council's massive survey of pupils who left at the minimum age. In the course of the interviews the early leavers, who were overwhelmingly working class, were given a long list of possible things the school could do and asked to say how important each of the things listed was to them personally. Topping the list was: 'Learning things that will help you to get as good a job or career as possible', which was rated as very important by 86 per cent of the boys and 88 per cent of the girls. In the present situation, then, education for many pupils has been emptied of its potential as a means of self-realization and has become primarily a medium of economic exchange. But things are changing and the balance is beginning to tip.

Up until now teachers and pupils have been more or less obliged to work with the materials produced by the big publishing companies, and consequently they have exercised little or no control over the content and presentation. The publishers' attempts to maximize profits by marketing books that can be used with a wide range of groups in a wide range of situations has often meant that the available materials were not particularly well suited to the needs of pupils in specific situations. The new technology of reproduction, however, reduces this dependence and makes it possible for teachers and pupils to produce material tailored to their particular interests and needs. Examples include the pamphlets compiled for the humanities courses in some of the Leicestershire schools, and the storybooks produced for younger boys by a group of fourth years in a Hackney school mentioned by Ken Worpole elsewhere in this volume. These sorts of innovations have two important effects. Firstly, they encourage pupils to develop and articulate their own particular sense of themselves and their situation, over and against the definitions imposed on them from outside. Secondly, by moving pupils out of their role as consumers and enabling them to become producers, these activities demystify the process of authorship and cut away at the dominant definition of 'cultural' production as something separate from everyday life and best left to the experts.

Nor are these activities necessarily peripheral. The Mode Three option provided under the CSE examination system gives teachers considerable control over the course content and assessment procedures so that work originated by pupils can contribute towards the certificate. This provides a way of increasing the intrinsic satisfaction which pupils derive from their school work while at the same time providing them with certificates which they can present to prospective employers. Given the current demand for certification by both pupils and employers, this provides a reasonable compromise with the contingencies of the present situation. If these sorts of innovations are to go beyond compromise, however, and to become the rule rather than the exception, the next step is to press for the mode three system to become an option for all pupils.

The dominant definition equates 'education' with what happens in schools and colleges and with the time people spend in these buildings. Education in this sense is assumed to stop at the school gates and to finish when people enter full-time employment. It is symptomatic, for example, that market researchers refer to the age at which people left school or college as their 'Terminal Education Age'. Against this is a view of education as a continuing process of self-realization and self-discovery, a dimension of lived experience. Once this alternative is accepted it follows that education cannot be synonymous with what goes on within the school walls, and that the environment must be regarded as a potentially rich source of educational experience. It involves a continual two-way traffic between the school and the surrounding community in which members of the school engage in action within the community and the school in turn provides a pool of resources which members of the community can draw upon in the course of extending their own educational experiences. In this way schools cease to be set apart and become involved in the aspirations of local people and in their continuing struggle for control over their own lives. This alternative definition of the role of schools in the educational process underpins the current community school experiments.

It is easy to overestimate the importance and influence of education and to assume that once education is changed everything else will fall into place, and class inequalities will quietly disappear. This is a mistaken view. In order to make a significant dent in inequalities it is necessary to change the distribution of wealth and property on which they rest. However, this does not mean that what happens within education is irrelevant. On the contrary, the sorts of changes mentioned here are important because they challenge dominant assumptions and open up alternative definitions of what is possible. Through their participation in these alternatives people may come to redefine what they expect and what they demand.

Educational change must therefore be seen as part of the wider struggle to create a society in which ordinary people can realize the range of their potentialities and recognize themselves as fully human in all their activities. In the present situation, where innovation is so often reduced to a problem of technique, it is all too easy to lose sight of this basic point. R. H. Tawney's eloquent reminder is therefore perhaps even more relevant now than when he first wrote it, just sixty years ago.

It is a very barren kind of pedantry which would treat education as though it were a closed compartment within which principles are developed and experiments tried undisturbed by the changing social currents of the world around. The truth is that educational problems cannot be considered in isolation from the aspirations of the great bodies of men and women for whose sake alone it is that educational problems are worth considering at all.

Educational change, then, is a wager on the future; a wager on people's continuing capacity to develop new ways of using resources and organizing relationships, and to struggle for the material means to put them into practice.

Reading Guide

The basic relations between culture, class and education are clearly laid out in chapters two and three of *Class Inequality and Political Order* by Frank Parkin (Paladin Paperback 1972). An interesting, but definitely more difficult extension of some of the same themes is provided by Louis Althusser's essay in B. Cosin (ed.) *Education: Structure and Society* (Penguin Books 1972). For an account of how these relations may look to a teacher see Chris Searle's *This New Season* (Calder and Boyars 1973).

5. The Invisible Ruling Class

Douglas Holly

A clear view of the class nature of our society can be obtained by studying the realities of its economic basis. But the idea of 'social class' as used by educationists is hardly ever clear. By and large educational journalists and even sociologists persist in talking as though it were all just a matter of different incomes, life-styles and tastes. Douglas Holly attempts to show how this prevents us from seeing what are the real controlling interests in Britain and how these really affect education. He challenges the popular idea that it is the middle classes who dominate the school system.

Born in 1930 Douglas Holly has taught the whole range of ability in secondary schools. He now works at Leicester University School of Education preparing graduate teachers for new approaches in comprehensive schools. He has written Society, Schools and Humanity (*MacGibbon and Kee, 1971*) *and* Beyond Curriculum (*Hart Davis MacGibbon, 1974*). *Both books are now available in Paladin paperbacks.*

The notion put about by many sociologists – particularly those who bring their talents to bear on the education system – is that we live in a two-class society. Education, they say, reflects this division. The working class, on the one hand, show only a limited interest in education and aren't much good at it. The parents fail to encourage their children at school or provide the right setting at home for educational success. They don't read many books and they watch the wrong sort of television. Their language, too, we are told, is all wrong for educational purposes since it doesn't put enough emphasis on words to convey meaning, relying instead on the shared understanding of people in close daily contact. The working class, except for a small group trying to get their children a better start in life, are, in fact, born educational failures.

The middle class, so the theory goes, are the other group in society. *They* take good care that *their* children suceed at school – so much so that, when it comes to higher education, eight out of ten students are still from middle class homes. By and large, schools are designed for the middle class and run by their representatives, the teachers. The way people are supposed to behave in schools, a large part of what they are supposed to learn, the goals they are supposed to strive for, all these things and more are custom-made for middle class children.

No wonder working class people aren't interested in education, say the sociologists: they can see the game is rigged against them. Where special schools are provided for the working class these have always been inferior – whether they were called 'elementary' or 'secondary modern'. Now that comprehensive schools are supposed to ensure equal education for all they are provided with different *courses* in the same school – the 'A stream' do academic subjects and the 'C stream' do 'Newsom' or RSLA'. In these circumstances the working class kids get cynical soon after they enter secondary school and just fool around, with or without their teachers' consent, until the longed-for day comes to leave. Failure for the working class is built into the system just as surely as success is for the middle class.

These Jeremiahs, however, miss one vital point. A class system which has a bottom and a middle but no top makes nonsense. How strange that we hear so much of the 'working' class and 'middle' class while we hear almost nothing about any 'upper' class. In what sense are the middle class people so powerful when they are apparently unable to prevent changes that – if the argument is true – must undermine their control? Streaming, for instance, is beginning to go. New approaches to learning encourage children to think for themselves rather than depend on the teacher for all the right answers. The way people behave is becoming more democratic with less kow-towing and more genuine friendliness between teachers and pupils. Learners are being encouraged to explore new areas of knowledge – including sociology – that are almost as much of a mystery to their teachers. Of course this isn't happening in *all* schools and it tends to be happening most in bright new schools in suburban areas where most of the inhabitants would be described by sociologists as middle class rather than working class. Nevertheless national curriculum developments aren't actually *forbidden* in city-centre schools or schools on large council estates – and not all children in suburban schools are middle class.

In fact, to understand the real situation in schools and the way changes come about we need to be much clearer about the actual class structure of society than sociologists of education usually are: we must, in fact, rediscover the missing class – the true ruling class, the one whose interests are *really* involved in keeping things as they are or changing them for this or that group of children in schools.

There is, first of all, no argument about the existence of a working class. But most sociologists are very vague about this group and tend to underestimate both its size and its significance. The working class is really, in a sense, nearly all of us. In terms of the known source and distribution of economic power a comparatively tiny group actually controls a huge proportion of privately owned wealth. Even when they go through the rigmarole of paying themselves salaries these people's power rests in their outright title to *ownership* of the wealth in question so that their earnings are hardly the point. Our society is a capitalist one – even a Tory Prime Minister admits it now – a society in which ownership and control of the means of production, distribution and exchange is claimed by a relatively small number of individuals. These capitalist owners constitute the really dominant class – the missing upper class. In relation to them the rest of us are all 'workers', in the sense that we all of us have to sell whatever labour-power we have in return for a wage or salary.

But, while the vast majority of people are actually employed in producing and distributing the wealth of society, there is a largish group engaged in managing these processes on behalf of the owners and controllers, making day-to-day decisions, studying and organizing technology, looking after health, culture, entertainment and legal problems and – not the least important – running the education system at its different levels. This is the well-known middle class. Although it tends to be a little fuzzy at the edges, its manner of existence is sufficiently different from that of either the ruling class or the working class to form a distinct group. In fact, though, like the sociologists, most working people don't see beyond this class at all: they see the middle class as the bosses.

But there are, in reality, strict limits to the power of people who are correctly described as middle class. From the point of view of ordinary working people the salaried staff in factories, for instance, really are the bosses, making all the decisions. They really have power after all in terms of, say, who does and doesn't get work. Yet these managers themselves know that they can only make decisions within limits laid down from above as company policy. The more thoughtful worker realizes that his real adversaries in the work situation are not the 'office boys' but the faceless men in the board rooms of London, Amsterdam, or New York.

In terms of education, again, the teachers and local administrators really have a great deal of day-to-day power. The sociologists' observation about the custom-made nature of much of what goes on in schools is correct as far as it goes. But just as the factory manager doesn't decide what commodities his factory will produce, the director of education and the headmaster don't usually decide the nature of what goes on as education: they take this for granted. Viewed by the pupil the teachers' powers seem absolute. The subject teacher decides exactly what he will teach every day in his class, the headmaster decides when subjects will be taught, which teachers will take them, even whether some subjects will be taught at all. The headmaster and teachers decide on the school rules, the headmaster and governors decide what clothes pupils may wear to school, even how long their hair should be. To the pupil, a headmaster may actually seem more like a prison governor than a factory manager. But the headmaster, and the prison governor too, have an authority which is absolute *only within limits laid down by others*. If the Home Office decides to turn a maximum security gaol into an open prison or the Ministry of Education decides to allow an academic grammar school to become fully comprehensive these power figures are seen as men of straw.

Even if we accept that total changes are not ordered in the nature of institutions every day, nevertheless school teachers have much less freedom of decision than they appear to from the pupils' point of view. One source of control usually quoted by teachers themselves is the examination system. It's all very well, they say, talking about freedom and democracy and pupil choice but in the end we have to get them through O-levels or CSE. It's the O-level and CSE Boards who really decide what happens in lessons. Even if all pupils don't go in for exams the books and equipment have to be bought according to the exam syllabus. Younger pupils have to be taught History and Geography in case they may one day want to take exams in these subjects. And so on. Of course, teachers are really being over-modest when they say that they have no control over the curriculum since, more and more, exams are becoming teacher controlled. There *are* schools where O-levels are taken on a school based syllabus and the exams reflect rather than decide what goes on in lessons. Nevertheless – and this is the important thing – teachers *feel* that they have little power of decision. Class teachers depend on the agreement of the headmaster to any changes in their relationships with exam bodies and headmasters often fear to make changes because of the reaction of parents, governors, inspectors and education officers. All this shows that, whatever ordinary working class parents may think, teachers themselves are far from feeling like bosses.

In terms of very important questions like *what* is taught and the methods employed, including, for instance, whether or not there shall be streaming by ability, it is legally teachers, especially headmasters, who make the decisions. But what really decides whether changes are going to be made or whether things are going to go on in much the same old way is a vague pressure which can only be called 'the climate of opinion'. Now, like the climate which determines our weather, this climate tends to operate differently in different places at different times. It controls the general *drift* of things without always allowing us to tell with much accuracy what will happen in any one place tomorrow. It all depends on local circumstances. In the county of Loamshire, perhaps, nothing much of importance has happened in any sphere for many years. The county council is run by aristocratic farmers and retired capitalists. One day the old director of education is replaced by a promising young man with excellent qualifications. The new man turns out to be quite a politician. Gradually he persuades the education committee that, since more money is available to them due to an expanding population, a new school plan is possible. Under this there is a quiet reorganization in which all the secondary modern schools become comprehensive and the eleven plus is phased out. The grammar schools are not 'abolished' but given new buildings and, in return for taking older students of all abilities, encouraged to develop new curricula. The plan, once set in motion, develops its own momentum. The 'climate of opinion' is against selection at eleven and this has gone. It now favours experiments which do away with streamed classes based on one or another test of ability and the experiments become standard practice. New curricula mean new teaching methods such as teachers working together in teams rather than as isolated individuals and pupils being given more responsibility. Much of what happens goes beyond what even the director had quite intended but the plan as a whole is admired. Local government reorganization comes along and the successful director takes charge of an enlarged area. The Labour Party aldermen of the city which now forms part of the new authority see their plan for 'comprehensivization' scrapped: the plan by which they have secretly hoped to preserve some of the much-favoured grammar schools as sixth-form colleges while leaving some of the old secondary moderns virtually unchanged, actually overturned by the Tories in favour of genuine comprehensive schools. Social

revolution advances over the inert bodies of social demo-
crats, its banners carried by the squirearchy. Nobody quite
knows how it all happened. Only the 'climate of opinion'
supplies any kind of explanation.

And this 'climate of opinion' is a will-o'-the-wisp which
flickers over the whole social situation, affecting behaviour
and policy in all sorts of spheres. It determines the frank-
ness or otherwise of public discussion about sex and
politics. It is behind attitudes to things like dress, pop
music, 'permissiveness'. It is in effect, the balance of power
between liberal and conservative ideas at any one moment.
It relates directly to the nature of momentarily influential
groups within the invisible ruling class. By and large the
conservative ideas, the Festival of Light reactions, the
pornography hunting, represent the influence of those
among the ruling class whose interests are most closely tied
to maintaining the surface of capitalist society as un-
ruffled as possible and who hate change of any sort. In any
case, attacks on vociferous 'lefty' students and university
academics, for whom popular support tends to be rather
weak, makes possible attacks on general militancy among
trade unionists. It is important for the preservation of the
system in general that the unions should be kept within
their acceptable role as harmless hagglers, politically dis-
armed. This role has recently shown signs of being rejected
by working people, with shipbuilders' work-ins, engineers
strengthening miners' picket lines and socialist ideas being
introduced into public discussion for the first time in a
generation. In these circumstances the influence of capitalism's sentinels has been quickly felt, not only in the
rapid enactment of tough police laws but also in the
widespread appearance of decency campaigns aimed
at putting the brake on progressive thinking of all
kinds.

On the other hand there is a strong interest on the part of

another wing of the ruling class in 'modernity'. Capitalism can no longer be content with the nuts and bolts of social life. As a condition of its existence it must expand or wither. Production must increase, so consumption must increase. New forms of consumption must be promoted to call forth new forms of production. Thus 'pop culture' of various sorts is encouraged – even if this means elevating working class people and interests and ways of life at the expense of the supposedly 'dominant' middle class. Ideas about exciting new techniques and technology are fostered even if this means scrapping Latin in schools in favour of 'creative design'. All is progress – or looks like it, anyway. The whole multi-million pound promotion industry, the entertainment industry, the fashion world are all aspects of capitalist expansion. Dour financiers in their City offices watch the teleprinter rather than the TV and beat music probably gives them a headache, but the fortunes of some of them are tied up in recording tape. A whole electronics industry depends on the sale of record players and transistor radios.

All of this represents a powerful vested interest in 'progress'. In America Ivan Illich decries the 'hidden curriculum of schools' which, he says, really teaches children the need to listen to others and promotes the false values of production merely for the sake of consumption. Strangely he concentrates his attack on schools and fails to mention the hidden programme of radio and television and the unprinted editorial policy of newspapers. The cry of Illich and others like him is 'de-school society!' This is like saying that by banning newspapers and broadcasting and allowing people to find out what's going on by word of mouth we will prevent the manipulation of ideas by the hidden rulers of society. The de-schoolers and those who rail against the media forget that working people, while they may feel powerless, are not simple. They *know* that passing exams isn't real education, that all they read in newspapers isn't gospel truth and that toothpaste isn't all you need for social confidence. Teachers and reformers and middle class people in general constantly insult the intelligence of the working class while overestimating their own freedom to enjoy a fulfilled human existence. As a result they busy themselves campaigning against pollution of the environment and other liberal minded causes while the faceless rulers of society go on unnoticed, quietly pursuing goals that will result in more and more pollution, the uprooting of human and animal populations, wars, famines and genocide. Capitalist enterprises even give money to support campaigns for famine relief, population control, wild life preservation and environmental purity. The Devil, it seems, is the most enthusiastic moralist of them all. You can be sure he is chairman of the board of any society against environmental pollution. The ruling class will actively support any reform and any progressive policy that doesn't actually reveal their power or suggest an alternative way of running things. Indeed, as I've already pointed out, they have a genuine *interest* – in the economic sense – in any form of modernization or 'daring new thinking' which may lead to some new form of consumption and, therefore, production. Oil barons, if they could only find a more lucrative source of energy to own, would shut down the oilfields tomorrow, sink all the giant tankers – with their crews if necessary – and promote legislation to outlaw petrol fumes. Capitalists are not interested in the form of commodity, only in the form of ownership and the size of economic return.

In the light of this we should hardly be surprised that the education system is seeing big changes. On the other hand we shouldn't expect too much either. Innovation we will see in plenty – new ways of learning, new things to learn, even new sorts of relationship between teachers and taught.

This is because the climate of opinion allows certain new things to happen which then develop according to their own laws. An approach to education which encourages active enquiry, questioning, self-sufficiency and co-operation among learners and between learners and teachers is bound to lead to more democratic regimes in schools. If teachers become used to discussing their plans among themselves and with their pupils they are scarcely going to tolerate stiff, autocratic attitudes in headmasters, inspectors or school governors. But powerful resistance is to be expected too. The Napoleons of knowledge aren't going to surrender without a fight: and they will get strong support from influential people. University professors will go on writing Black Papers, Tory MPs will try hard to prevent schools in their constituencies from teaching about the Russian Revolution, local busybodies will organize worried parents to stop the rot. We may even see a period of reaction in which the more insecure among the middle class will regain control and enforce conformity. Police action is necessary from time to time to warn some people not to go too far. The laws of conspiracy now being developed could no doubt be deployed against teachers as well as trade unionists.

It is best to see developments in social agencies like the education system as a narrow balance of forces always liable to shift one way or the other. Both the progressive forces and the reactionary ones are in the end dependent on the interests of the mysterious rulers of society, who are so modest that they don't show themselves often – and even when they do, never as *rulers*. In fact it doesn't matter if they don't even know *themselves* that they are rulers: the processes of social and economic power don't depend on any vast conspiracy or even awareness of power by the ruling class. They may themselves believe quite sincerely – some of them – that they are humble subjects of a democracy, just like their workpeople and managers. After all the laws of England are made by a sovereign Parliament duly elected by the people, the majority of whom are wage earners or small salary earners. From time to time we have a Labour government which introduces all sorts of revolutionary measures like increased pensions, free false teeth and heavy taxes on those with high incomes. In such a society no one can live any longer like an eastern potentate, no one can do as he likes.

But that isn't the point. Capitalism doesn't depend on capitalists being able to do as they like – in fact, quite the reverse. In the 1930s the whole system nearly collapsed because of the greed and unruliness of individual capitalists. Just in time the more responsible got together and, knowing that the system was more important than any individual's profit, agreed to accept restraint, enlightened social policies and the independent power of the state. Modern capitalism still stands subject to these rules, national and international. Just so long, anyway, as the state doesn't become *too* independent – that is, cease to represent their basic interests – and democracy doesn't become real – that is demand too much control over the all-important ownership of material resources and labour-power. Capitalists usually prefer to keep out of politics – a ruling class in fact but not in name. They are even delighted to do business with communist states and accept, even promote, co-existence and co-operation between East and West. But just as it is one thing to be soft on communism abroad but quite another to allow the growth of socialism at home, so it is within the individual institutions of our benevolent capitalist society. 'Progressive' developments in schools are to be encouraged, especially when they chime in with the growth of new forms of consumption, but 'progressives' in education need to be kept an eye on. This doesn't mean that there is some secret inner cabinet which meets to decide

how the English education system should work in the
interests of international capitalism. Nothing so simple.
The matter is best seen as a constantly shifting movement
of interests with now this face of capitalism visible, now
that – and each of them, of course, acceptable. At one time
the emphasis is on progress. We hear a lot from the Bow
Group Tories. There is legislation to prevent homosexuals
from being persecuted and black people from being discriminated against. Experiments in education are applauded.
A month or so later reaction sets in again: The Monday
Club Tories are in the ascendant. Newspapers are full of
crimes committed by young people. Immigrants are
declared illegal after years of residence. There is legislation
against trade unions, and experimental schools are said to
have gone too far.

But though there are variations in the temperature and
barometer readings are erratic, the climate of opinion
remains the same. On the whole the pressures exerted by
our self-effacing ruling class are in the direct of social
progress – in the narrower sense, anyway. There are *real*
advances in education, some of which have been mentioned.
For people entering the teaching profession this is both an
exciting and a trying time. It's exciting because there are
great possibilities for work in and out of the classroom
which is meaningful and which allows young people in
school to develop insight and understanding. It's trying
because of continuing frustrations, obstacles put in your
way by older teachers who are uncomfortable with the new
ideas and headmasters who are really only half convinced,
difficulties with parents sometimes – not least the uncertainty of students themselves who find it unbelievable that
anything interesting and pleasant can be serious work.
There is also a lot to be done by teachers before new
approaches are fully worked out so that they are not only
better than the old mumbo-jumbo but truly *education* –

systematic and satisfying, a realization for all people of what lies within them. Though that may sound utopian it's a necessary goal, and one not completely unattainable – in principle. The climate of opinion favours this development in so far as it favours experiment and new developments in general.

Of course there comes a point where the degree of progress encouraged in our society shows itself as a mirage. Developments are encouraged for their novelty not for their real worth. There is no system about the innovations that are introduced, neither a system of liberation nor one of repression. The only real principle is the principle of free enterprise: new ideas must lead to there being some economic gain for someone in the end – or at least show promise of doing so. Teachers, parents and others involved in education need to sift new ideas carefully so that the worthwhile can be sorted from the merely trendy. Teachers in particular need to accept the professional responsibility of *building* a system where none exists. They need to discover the real principles of education – to discover which ideas are basic and help people to go on learning and improving their understanding and human feeling, what methods are most likely to encourage this to happen, how they can get their students to co-operate in their own development. Parents too need to see beyond their own experience of schools and what was often miscalled education to something more basic that their children are struggling towards. They need to recall what they always instinctively knew – that true education isn't just something dry and dead that goes on in dusty classrooms, only useful for giving you a start in life – it *is* life, or a large part of it anyway. It's learning not only the principles of science but what lies behind science, the possibility of men and women understanding and controlling their own lives – not only the physical universe but the social system as well.

Education, in fact, is the only thing that will make democracy possible in the end, since it involves not only *understanding* more but developing *feelings* that are not animal and destructive but human and 'moral' in the real sense of the word.

Though the progressive climate of opinion which tends to hold sway most of the time can lead to important changes in schools it can't lead to this because its origin lies in the selfish interests of a ruling class. The economic system which gives rise to capitalists, however modern and progressive and permissive, is essentially anti-human. Once it served a purpose: it allowed men and women to escape from the tyranny of ignorance. By harnessing the surplus mental and physical labour-power of people it opened the possibility of overcoming the dominance of nature, it showed us the vision of a *human* world. But this harnessing under capitalism remains the means of personal enrichment for the few, the invisible ones. The ambition of capitalists is a narrow, pathetic ambition. Instead of pleasure it brings bitterness even to the owners of wealth. By its denial of a full humanity to the mass of people it brings frustration, squalor and – to millions throughout the world – actual suffering. The exploitation is not a human exploitation of the earth's resources but an irresponsible exploitation of nature – and of men. The only law capitalism knows is the law of its own survival – and there is no guarantee that it will be able to obey even that with the technology now at its disposal. It is even possible that it will destroy itself by destroying human existence altogether.

The alternative to all this is clear and has been for a long time. People need to take over their own destiny. The co-operative labour-power of men and women needs to be democratically disposed of so that things happen because they are to everyone's advantage. This is why education is so vital, because ordinary people the world over need to develop an intelligence and sensitivity far greater than that of the present rulers. It's a tall order, but no taller than other goals that men have set themselves, like exploring the universe or harnessing the power of the atomic nucleus. The difficulty lies not in the problem faced while making the attempt but in the opposition that can be expected from those whose dominance and control is challenged by it. And this ruling minority has always been able to depend on lackeys who see themselves diminished by a human existence for others. Whatever displeases the ruling class, whatever threatens their secret interests is sure to call forth a host of apologists for the world as we have it now. Already there are psychologists who tell us that whole races of men are genetically stupid, that the mass of people lack the biological possibility of growing mentally. The ordinary man has to be content with the dream of getting a bit more like Mr Universe, the ordinary woman with the dream of sharing a little of Miss World's charms. Not for them the model of a Mr or Miss Intelligence. That's reserved for the lucky few whose IQ tops the 130 mark – according to tests carefully devised by other clever people, good at puzzles and word games. Then there are philo-sophers of knowledge who explain that real understanding is so fantastically complex, depends on so much very rare learning of out of the way ideas, that only a few lucky people – like them – can hope to be truly educated. Others should be content with enjoying life physically – Mr Universe and Miss World again – and expressing them-selves picturesquely in one way or another. The culture of 'the folk', they believe, also has its worth – in its own kind of way. Finally there are the sociologists – the Jeremiahs referred to earlier – who can demonstrate the hopelessness of the situation for ordinary people. They don't take too seriously those ideas about genetically inherited intelligence based on experiments with rats in mazes and pigeons in cages nor the high-class talk of the philosophers. But they do explain how the cards are stacked by environmental factors and the thinking habits of working class people who are their own worst enemies, refusing to profit by help when it *is* offered and preferring the comfort of their familiar domination. These sociologists are progressives: they believe that all this can be changed gradually if only we can wait for the leadership of a few working class people who – like them – have managed to win through in spite of it all. They advise people to be suspicious about more revolutionary ideas, however. These tend to be the work of renegades from the middle class who have never known privation or what it is to be working class – so how can they know what's really good for working class people? Which is rather like saying that someone who's never known a day's illness in his life shouldn't presume to study medicine.

Again, there's no conspiracy here. These people in colleges and universities aren't secret agents actually hired by the ruling class to fend off social revolution. Their fears are real and shared by many other middle class people – particularly those who have only recently got into the middle class by succeeding in the education system. There is no doubt that being in the middle class is more comfortable than being a wage earner. You have more of a feeling of being your own boss and more real freedom of action. Professional jobs especially offer the chance of personal reward and fulfilment quite apart from a comfortable financial situation. Who wouldn't want to defend these privileges in a mean world? Any change in the way society is organized looks like a threat to some middle class people. If the school system seems to work in a way that suits you, why ask questions about real education? These feelings are as true for people working in universities as for any others. Consequently it comes as no surprise to find so many taking a conservative or reformist position. The sort of philosophy or sociology or economics which asks searching questions tends to be thought of as theoretical, a sort of leisured man's game. When it comes to practical concerns like education or social work such questions are forgotten, the main consideration being how to make things work better *now*, in the society we've got. After all, we know what the day-to-day problems are well enough – overcrowded classrooms, too little money being spent on books and equipment, backwardness in reading and mathematical skills, lack of motivation to do well. There's enough to be done here, without dreaming about changing the nature of education and even society!

Such a point of view is easily understandable but totally wrong. It is really a way of saying 'we're powerless'. The middle class, in the end, feel even less control over their own destiny than the working class – perhaps because they're one step nearer the real source of power. Middle class people tend to devote every leisure moment to making their existing life even more comfortable and rewarding, recognizing the limits within which they are bound by society. Their private lives become a total preoccupation, leaving no room for thoughts about the need to be real human beings in charge of their own and their children's future. Such freedom, they think, is a pipe dream fit for unpractical revolutionaries and visionaries. Their knowledge of how the social system works convinces them that it is eternal and unchangeable. Most of them refuse to believe in the ruling class and the hard facts of economic power. While they don't see themselves as the bosses, as the workers think of them, they accept that they are in a comfortable and desirable situation compared with most working class people – though they tend also to deny any great gap and even say that wage earners are better off, having almost as much money for far less worry. They all believe that we live in a democracy where there are no rulers except those duly elected every five years. Having very little understanding of how wealth is created, they have no idea of surplus labour-power and the significance of who owns it. They seem to believe it all grows on trees and that the only argument possible is how to share it out the fairest way. They will defend their larger incomes by claiming to have earned them by having better brains or having striven harder. The workers they say are really lazy and envy the fruits of harder work and greater intelligence.

There is no hope then of the middle class being much interested in critical thinking about the way things are organized. Their reaction to change is likely to be either suspicion or uncritical enthusiasm for bright new machinery and techniques of doing things. They greatly favour management approaches to education which improve the efficiency of delivering the goods. They never think of asking what these goods really are. Their support can be counted on for 'modern' developments. When it comes to deeper questions they will be less enthusiastic, even hostile. In this way the middle class acts, whether they know it or not, as the willing tool of vested interests, the interests of a ruling class which they don't even believe exists. In education as in other matters affecting the way society runs, they are the agents of conservatism or superficial change. As parents some eagerly attend school meetings and form committees to buy extra equipment. In general they support whatever the teachers suggest, especially where this involves being more progressive and up to date. These are the liberals. In social policy as in politics they believe in making society more democratic without changing its basis. Some of them belong to Fabian groups and vote Labour at elections. Most work eagerly for the Liberal party. Taken together they are the minority. The majority is conservative – with or without the big 'C'. These are suspicious of teachers, especially young ones. They will give money for cricket pavilions but aren't interested in discussing education. On the whole what was good enough for them is good enough for their children. They believe in hard work, and competition, they say, is good for young people. Children should learn to work for cups and prizes and exam passes. It prepares them for the real world outside. If they won't work, won't compete, so much the worse for them.

Against all this, the friends as well as the enemies, those who believe in a new and different idea of education in schools must expect to contend. Since democracy and human progress in education – or anywhere else – can't be achieved by secret plotting but must, sooner or later, depend on the support of the mass of people, a big job of education, in another sense, lies ahead. People need to be persuaded that the schools can serve *them*. Teachers must be encouraged to fight for genuine democracy, to involve working class and middle class students alike in a new and *real* type of learning. Parents, especially wage earners, must be shown that *their* kids matter and that the schools belong to *them*, not to the government – and certainly not to the great multi-national companies. They need to be reminded that education is interesting and worthwhile, an activity not a thing, an activity that needn't stop at sixteen. Pensioners as well as teenagers need education and can benefit from it. We can't stop being educated while we live. The fruits of what we learn will be enjoyed by generations unborn. In the end the rulers can't win – they can't be allowed to. Humanity has a trick of surviving its own excesses, including those of its rulers. But it won't happen by itself – and it may be touch and go for some time to come. The invisible rulers must first be made visible so that we can all see where our interests really lie. Only then can they be moved aside in favour of a society not divided against itself by class interests based on an undemocratic exercise of economic power. Education and enlightenment is both the means of achieving this and the outcome of that achievement.

6. Integrating Art into Society

Ian Jeffrey

The impoverished definitions of culture which have been foisted on ordinary people in our society have inevitably resulted in confusion and a sense of inadequacy. This is one way in which the rulers maintain their superiority – by making it seem that only they have the key to understanding the finer things in life. Nowhere is this more so than in the world of art. Ian Jeffrey notes the connection between the attempt to see art as a scarce commodity to be hoarded in galleries and collections and the way in which schools fail to bridge the gap between pupils' creative efforts and their critical awareness of their surroundings.

Ian Jeffrey, born in 1942, has himself been involved in the battle of opposing interest groups which beset art colleges in 1968. He briefly lost his job, dismissed as a militant. He now lectures in the History of Art at Goldsmith's College, University of London. His particular research interest is popular art and photography. He is the author of A Social History of Photography, *due to be published shortly by Studio Vista.*

The sheer variety of art now on display, exhibited or in picture books, may stimulate the growth of the notion that art is a type of undemanding entertainment, an attractive passing show, in competition with and sharing the nature of television and the cinema but at a somewhat more prestigious level. The degree of understanding required to participate in this sort of passing show is fairly slight; it is sufficient to attend and, in the case of an exhibition, to purchase the catalogue or commemorative booklet. The willing spectator or consumer of art books and exhibitions is certainly a major factor in the present art scene; the unending parade of exhibitions and revivals of a multitude of neglected artists and forgotten styles suggests that, no matter how carefully researched the catalogue notes may be, this sort of activity stems from a view of art as quickly changing entertainment placing a high value on the novel and the unexpected.

The 'consumer' certainly comes into contact with the material on which an understanding can be based but, in view of the variety of art styles brought onto the stage and as suddenly removed, is unlikely to develop penetrating insights into any of the particular pieces presented to him. The process of presentation and promotion is such as to convert art objects into items of fashion, of little more than seasonal interest.

Perhaps it would be better to turn for a model towards those who promote and present art: they have the knowledge of the evolution of style and subject matter and the acquaintance with a sufficient range of art objects to identify and to analyse works of art. However, their refined skills can be learned and mastered only through a constant familiarity and traffic with works of art; in view of the relative scarcity of such objects and their concentration in a few hands these are not skills learned by many. Specialists of this sort are a mandarin group delighting in their mastery of the secret places and byways of art. It is a closed profession and a remunerative one in which the ability to make correct attributions can be well rewarded. Its responsibilities are towards a limited group of collectors or towards their institutional counterparts, the museums. There is a certain sort of understanding involved here and it is a very refined one. The misfortune is that such hard won skill tends to be so jealously guarded, to be placed at the service of such limited interests, and to form the basis of a privileged caste of narrow responsibilities.

Yet, ideally, this sort of detailed knowledge of works of art can be used to stimulate a much more general under-standing of the visual arts. This is epitomized by Philip Rawson's book *Drawing* in the *Appreciation of the Arts* series (OUP 1969). Where art historians habitually exercise their skills in narrowly defined areas he adapts their proce-dures for use across a wide range of subject matter, ana-lysing the problems of representation common to most figurative art. He refers to both Indian and European drawing, for instance, studies the relations of line and ground, line and picture field, and compares the effects of varying materials in drawing. Instead of concentrating on style identification, as is customary in this area of study, this is an analysis of process; eventually it can lead to the development of an ability to compare all sorts of artefacts one with another, rather than merely checking a limited number of art objects against a style concept such as Baroque or Classical. Through an approach such as this many more types of objects than previously admitted come within the scope of analysis, from the cartoons and news photos in the daily press to book covers and adver-tising posters. Such an approach will not necessarily sim-plify the business of looking at art – in many cases it can make it more difficult – but it will extend consciousness into areas which we generally regard as being too banal to excite attention. Ultimately it should alert us to a whole range of composed images in the press and on television which we tend to regard innocently as nothing more than reflections of reality, when in fact they are as carefully and purposively engineered as the most sophisticated painting.

This open approach to the analysis of the visual arts runs

counter to the assumption that there is a restricted corpus
of paramount works of art which alone merit study. It is
assumed in art history, for instance, that most Italian
church art of the seventeenth century is intrinsically of high
quality. This may well be so, but for as long as it is treated
as a closed system the claim is one which cannot be tested.
The more open art appreciation becomes, the more likely
we are to be able to assess the traditionally esteemed categories of art, to discover if they are esteemed out of anything more substantial than an inherited pattern of study.

If Philip Rawson's book *Drawing* is a more productive
example for art education than, for instance, one of the
British Museum catalogues of Italian drawings it is equally
obvious that both depend in their different ways on first-
hand knowledge of art objects. In both cases it is often
difficult to follow the exposition of an idea by reference to
the book illustrations alone. Not only are reproductions
insufficiently accurate but they fail to convey much of the
authentic substance of a work of art. It is not just a question of authenticity of colour or a sense of scale but of the
absence of that authoritative call to attention which the
work of art makes when seen face to face. This sort of
direct acquaintance with art is central to its understanding;
it alone provides the stimulus to that attention and enthusiasm which are crucial to successful teaching. Books,
transparencies and film provide no more than a record of
the object: they function as support for first hand knowledge. Invariably they have to be interpreted and they often
provide just one more barrier between the spectator and
the object. We also have to guard against the fact that
reproduction of painting and sculpture is a form of
miniaturization, rendering much that is awesome and
impressive in reality, domestic and manageable in its
photographed form. It is in this way that art, which is by
definition special, declines to the level of everyday life,

E

taking its place as just another leisure activity. This process is probably the principal means of depreciating art and the more we can reduce our dependence on it the better.

If we are to escape from our vicarious consumption of art images we must return to the reality of actual paintings and sculptures. At the moment not only are people dependent on secondary sources for much of their knowledge of art but they appear to prefer this: to judge from the popularity of the postcard counters in the major galleries it seems that visitors turn with more assurance and attention to the reproduction than to the work itself. This stems, in part, from the way in which these major galleries have been assimilated into patterns of tourism, both providing focal points in an itinerary and giving assurances that tourism is fundamentally a serious business.

So, although more people are seeing more art than at any time in the past they are doing so in the odd circumstances of cultural tourism where the museum visit is not necessarily an end in itself but a means of legitimating the wider activity. It is a consequence of this that metropolitan museums are as crowded as railway termini whereas many excellent provincial galleries are all but deserted. The inspection of art under these conditions can only be cursory and the museums themselves are doing little to disrupt the pattern. Very often they ensure that their exhibits are difficult to comprehend: to see room after room of paintings dating from the European middle ages through to the early part of this century can easily lead to a thorough confusion on the part of most visitors. Seen in such profusion the works vie for attention when, in fact, they most repay prolonged examination item by item and free from the distraction of passing spectators. More seriously, from the point of view of a real understanding of art, the works themselves are generally exhibited in a most uninformative way. They are bereft of any context which might reflect on their original use or status: galleries display but they do not explain. Although projected as an educational institution an art gallery is more likely to function as a combination of public park and trophy room, a sort of open treasure house manifesting national potency; this is one way of explaining the extraordinary furore raised whenever the Americans, for instance, try to snare one of our national art treasures.

Museums tend to make a fairly sharp distinction between displaying their collections and providing information on the history of art. The objects they put on show usually reflect nothing more than contemporary notions on the formal evolution of painting; emphases change in accordance with fashionable revivals and the museum scarcely ever shows the connections between works of art and the society in which they were made and collected. Anyone visiting the Tate Gallery might see a certain amount of Victorian painting but would certainly learn nothing of the overall pattern of collecting in that period. The visitor might see examples of British painting carried out over the past twenty years but without being given any information on the premises underlying the selection of these works rather than others. In effect, the visitor is being exposed to a particular, and highly selective, version of the evolution of British art, one which ignores huge areas of activity from amateur painting to successful popular art; what is on display is nothing more than the taste of an avant-garde elite presented as a definitive history of art.

A museum is certainly the place to exercise an understanding of art, but hardly where such an understanding can be developed. This is not entirely the fault of museum administrations who have, in fact, inherited the idea that their public collections are private collections on a large scale: this attitude is so deep rooted and so closely involved with the present high exchange value of works of art that it cannot be seriously altered in the immediate future. These limitations must be clearly recognized so that any potential museum visitor can take advantage of the work which is put on show. This can only happen if all of us have preliminary experience of art works. There are a number of ways in which this can be achieved including a government sponsored public works programme to place major examples of contemporary painting and sculpture in our cities and alongside the motorways; even if the work was of poor quality it might encourage people to think about a broad social role for the visual arts. The crucial preparatory step, however, is to make actual art objects the basis for teaching in secondary education and to cut down on the reliance on massive inventories of colour transparencies and glossy colour plates. Some of the vast reserve collections in our museums and galleries could well be used for this purpose, although this might entail unacceptable risks and high insurance payments. Even within the range of contemporary art any educational authority could build up interesting teaching collections of graphic work, of good photography and amateur painting for a fraction of the price which might have to be spent on prestigious high art. If the skills of looking and analysing are to be developed it is at this point that the process should start, with fundamental and actual art objects no matter how modest.

Should local authorities build up this sort of collection as an aid to teaching, as a way of minimizing the vicarious consumption of art, the consequences could be considerable. Work could be purchased from students themselves, thus giving far more point to their activity than presently is the case. It might encourage the growth of a small scale and relatively manageable art at the expense of the inflated institutional scale popular since American painting swept to fame in the late 1950s. Not only should this put a greater range of art into circulation but do so in a way which would persuade artists that theirs is a useful and essential public role; in many cases this realization could well be inspirational for an artist presently uncertain of the ultimate destination of his work. Once familiar with the actuality of art works in an everyday context many people would wish to continue such an association, seeing them as an essential and integral part of any architectural project, as things to be seriously considered and generally owned and made. This is in no way to argue for the degradation of art, rather for its increased public accessibility.

One of the major checks to the development of such an integration lies in the very complexity of the conventions governing everything from landscape painting to the film poster. Although it is relatively easy to identify styles and schools of work, to distinguish Impressionism from Art Nouveau, Fauve painting from Cubism, it is quite another thing to say exactly how paintings differ under these various conventions. An individual teacher working in isolation is capable of explaining no more than a small proportion of accessible art; if this includes contemporary work the difficulties are accentuated by the concurrence of diverse and competing styles and attitudes. The problem can be solved by, for instance, moving towards a much greater integration of study. There should certainly be no real separation between the teaching of history and art history, and art history itself cannot be comprehended without some experience in the making of objects. At the moment there is probably a tacit resistance to this among art historians who see their discipline as running parallel to economic and social studies, but as something nobler and cleaner than either. One way in which this sort of integration can be achieved is through the study of local history which can perfectly well include research into local patronage, into the commissioning of war memorials, stained glass and civic statuary, for example.

It is perhaps even more crucial that the existing skills throughout the educational system should be put to better use. Within colleges and universities there are artists and art historians who scarcely ever teach outside their own particular institutions and even less frequently in other areas of art education. There is hardly any interaction between the various levels in the system. Each level in art education dedicates itself to a fresh start, either disregarding or actively trying to eliminate the lessons learned at the preceding level. Implicit in this process is a contempt for the preparatory stages in art teaching or a belief in fundamental differences of aim at each stage. Equally it reflects the overall compartmentalization of teaching in which there is no aim held in common, but a series of groupings who attend resolutely to their own interests.

Whatever the explanation, this prevailing stratification can be reduced and the personnel of the different areas encouraged into a greater sense of community and common purpose. It is probably impossible to do this on the basis of a shared set of beliefs which would give a coherency to the entire process. A common aim implies basic premises for the whole activity and fundamentalism of this sort would be very much at odds with, say, the design school which concentrates on encouraging a receptivity to fashionable trends as the passport to success.

Even a relatively straightforward attempt to integrate school and college would bring immediate advantages for both areas. It would ensure that school work helps rather than hinders the programmes of the Foundation Year courses in art colleges. If teaching artists were expected to exhibit and to explain their work in schools both the artist and his work might become better known and go far to counterbalance the established image of the artist as media hero, entertainer and celebrity. The prevalence of this sort of image of the artist does nothing but harm proposing, as it does, a model of conduct only open to one or two practi-tioners at any one time; scarcity value dictates that only a very few performers can be subject to this treatment at any particular time. The fact is that the vast porportion of art students will eventually become teachers of art where their work can be of maximum value to society. Anything which obscures this basic fact sets up false objectives and spreads confusion at a point where clarity is of the essence.

Indeed, one of the most conspicuous features of recent thinking on art education has been the stress placed on the need for an understanding founded on a more patient analysis and discussion than has hitherto taken place. Under the proposed terms art in school is no longer to be simply a matter of using art materials, but is to be con-siderably supplemented by an effort to understand its social and historical context. Art education has a responsibility to those who will form the audience and, the argument goes, as the vast proportion of students will become audience rather than practitioners the greater emphasis in teaching should go on the promotion of understanding. This case is most recently and cogently stated by Brian Allison in an extremely interesting essay 'Sequential Programming in Art Education: a Revaluation of Objectives' (in *Readings in Art and Design Education*, Vol. 1, ed. D. W. Piper, 1973).

Now, the case against too great a reliance on practice as the key to enjoyment and understanding is a formidable argument in favour of change, but one which needs to be carefully stated. A more complete diagnosis is that of Dick Field in *Change in Art Education* (1970). He argues that the major failure is in the secondary area which students leave without having acquired any coherent idea of art. The most telling index of failure he sees is the fairly general cessation of any art activity after leaving school. He thinks that at the secondary level art education is dominated by a faith in spontaneity inherited from the primary stage when drawing and painting are seen as part of a natural process of ordering experience. The trouble is that, once established, this idea is not seriously questioned even when children are no longer able to make art so naturally. As a result there is a reaction against explicit teaching and a failure to cultivate the idea that art processes can and have to be learned if painting and sculpture are to be anything other than the by-product of art therapy. This depreciates the idea of art and gives students a false impression which further decreases the chance of understanding and sympathy. This, Field argues, should be rectified by teaching art to do justice to its complexity and difficulty; eventually the child should stand some chance of being able 'to develop a coherent view of art or to think or talk adequately about it'.

Field's approach to art education judges present performance against the highest possible standards: he proposes an ideal system which is based on the identification of the positive counterparts to the defects in the present system. Instead of a nebulous, weakly held view of art the student is to aim for a coherent view; he proposes a maintenance rather than a lapse of interest in the years after education and instead of ignorance there is to be understanding. While this helps to identify an ideal model for art education it enumerates rather than explains the defects in the present system. It is admirable to call for an enhanced understanding of art and it should be possible to teach towards this, given perceptive and articulate teachers. Certainly, to recognize this need is to go some way towards creating a new consciousness. And yet the request comes at a time when there is, and has been for some time, a virtual industry devoted to the promotion of art and of art history. Throughout this century art publishing has furnished books on every conceivable type and interpretation of art, we have an increasing number of accessible galleries with their attendant specialist lecturers, and recently, with the development of colour television, large numbers of art educational films have appeared. Notwithstanding this widespread dissemination of images and information it seems that there remains a widespread failure to understand art, particularly amongst those most exposed to its examples and its literature. By stressing the persisting reliance on art practice both writers imply that these abundant secondary sources are not being put to full use, but can this be the full explanation?

It is necessary, after all, to consider why, in such a richly endowed situation, practically based art education has survived at the expense of teaching based on example and criticism. Perhaps teachers are correct, after all, to believe that understanding follows practice? This is an idea to which most artists hold fast and one which will certainly be maintained in schools, where teachers have been trained as fine artists. Nor is this an unfounded belief: the best art critic in Britain since the war, Patrick Heron, is primarily a painter; the extremely influential Roger Fry practised as an artist as, more recently, did Adrian Stokes. It could be claimed that art education is, in this respect, fundamentally correct and that its example should be more widely followed, that students of literature, for instance, should write as poets and novelists in order to gain richer insights into their area of study. Nevertheless, the sort of practice which serves Roger Fry or Patrick Heron cannot be equated with practice as it is currently interpreted in the context of the school classroom where it is patently ineffective in promoting an understanding either sufficiently wide or sufficiently deep. The source of this ineffectiveness is inadequate control and direction. Field asserts this when he regrets the decline of exercises in art in favour of an acceptance that anything done in the art room is definable as art work. Real art is difficult and its techniques have to be learned before it can be practised; but it is not necessarily the same sort of learning required for an academic subject. The trouble is that the sustained attentiveness required to learn how to draw or to paint cannot easily be achieved in the crowded circumstances of a school timetable and teachers are inevitably forced into compromises, particularly that of relying simply on the spontaneous creativeness of the child, even when that has been clearly outgrown. The instinct to rely on practice is, though well founded, difficult to effect. For what exactly does a practical understanding of art entail? Certainly, practice in drawing and painting introduce a student to all sorts of problems of representation in a way which is much more real than anything which could be achieved by explanation and discussion. The role of colour in painting, for instance, can best be understood through practice; its importance is invariably minimized in art history and criticism and its rendering in coloured reproductions always inaccurate. Probably the only way, for example, in which paintings by Bonnard and Sickert (both painters fond of schematic systems of colouring) could be understood, short of bringing their work into the classroom, would be by carrying out an exercise which involved using Bonnard's zonal colour arrangements or Sickert's facetted modelling pattern. This is one sort of understanding of a particular type of picture and it can probably only be arrived at through careful scrutiny of the work in question or through exercises based on that particular type of painting. It might be termed a physical understanding of art.

Not only, then, should institutional boundaries between teachers at different levels be less final than they are at the moment, but the complexity of art should be recognized by involving a greater number of practising artists and interpreters at the secondary school level; and this is another very good reason for encouraging the interaction of colleges and the school art departments. In addition it might allow the art treacher to devote more of his time to the practice in which he has been trained; it seems illogical to ask painters and sculptors who have trained and vested considerable hopes in their art to devote their entire time to teaching. This exclusive focus would not be expected of someone teaching in an art college and it is inconsistent to think that things are any different in a school where, in fact, the demands on a teacher might be greater and the need for individual expression on his part more rather than less necessary. This could be achieved if more part-time teaching posts were created, and if it resulted in an increase in the number of actively creative teachers it would be all to the good. For, if art teaching is going to lay such a stress on the priority of practice it is quite evidently unjust to deprive teachers of the time and the means to practise themselves! One proposal which might help towards solving such a problem, and at the same time help reinforce the connection between school and college, is to integrate post-graduate studies of art more closely with the schools. At the moment bursaries are granted without much being demanded in return; they ought to be made dependent on the student spending a brief period each year displaying and discussing his work in the schools of the authority from which he draws his bursary. This seems preferable to the present practice which merely results in the student's increasingly individualistic isolation within the art world, quite oblivious to any broader social responsibility. Not only does this establish the necessary links between schools and colleges and encourage the traffic of ideas, but it should serve as a considerable stimulus to resident teachers. This proposal which could have far-reaching consequences amounts to little more than extending to the schools the pattern of part-time teaching already familiar in the art colleges.

But even if we can secure a new integration through the movement of people there is still no absolute assurance that it will produce an enhanced understanding of art. In the first place, there are certain well established patterns of activity which are inimical to understanding as envisaged by a reformer such as Field. There are artists like Warhol and Hockney who are known through the media; they are talking points, but as personalities rather than artists. It is true that they may make use of their public image as a means of reflecting on the promotional aura in which their work is submerged, but ultimately this is little more than an equivocal mockery of our present time, as much an accommodation of the media as a criticism. Works of art are even less discussed and then only in a limited number of newsworthy ways, if stolen, sold at a record price or attacked by fanatics.

Recognizing the sensational and short-term nature of public attention, at least in the version projected by the popular press, some artists have cultivated a taste for the ephemereal and vulgar; inevitably this has produced a reaction in the other direction, towards the austere and the difficult – this is the transition from Pop Art to Minimalism in the 1960s. This quickly evolving pattern of movement and counter-movement has had important consequences. More than at any time in the past contemporary high art is completely absorbed in an internal dialogue, often so private as to exclude any but a small band of devotees. In many cases artists have adopted the mannerisms and some of the attitudes of logicians, aesthetics and philosophers and this has resulted in a style of activity absolutely alien to that of the painter and sculptor. The result is a rift, not only within the community of artists, but between practitioner and any sort of audience other than immediate colleagues. We are, then, living in conditions where the gap between contemporary practice and public understanding of that practice is widening. As a result interpretation has become rooted more firmly than ever in the hands of professional art watchers, agents and apologists.

The manifest difficulties involved in understanding modern art have resulted in widespread institutionalization: responsibility for the recognition and acclaim of art has passed into the hands of committees or teams of experts who purchase for collections and nominate to international exhibitions. It is this sort of recognition which is most sought by artists as the ultimate assurance of quality. Paintings are not bought by individual patrons so much as by corporations advised by experts, just as racing stock might be bought on the advice of trainers and breeders. The underlying motive in both cases is the search for success and prestige, acclaim in the eyes of posterity. Contemporary picture collections are not put together for reasons of personal delight; rather they are directed externally towards the general public or employee or client as audience; fundamentally they are indices of cultural respectability.

The effect of this process is to establish art as a profession like any other, and to promote a general reliance on the skills and services of the expert. It is the role of the audience to act as the passive recipients of this imposed taste, to accept decisions regarding good taste and generally to act as consumers. It is remarkable that the choice of work for public exhibitions, for civic centres and university refectories is so consistently questionable yet so rarely questioned. If this absence of challenge arises from anything it is from our lack of any developed means of talking about art, and it is this presumably what Field has in mind when proposing his reforms.

There is no shortage of example for an intelligent understanding of art. But what is often lacking is evaluative analysis; this means that examples of painting and sculpture are described, often minutely, but without indicating why one example or class of art is more significant or better than another. Criticism and history generally rest content with existing evaluations and whilst this may be justified in the stylistic analysis of High Renaissance altarpieces it is less useful in an evaluation of contemporary work. Even when a critic such as Max Raphael, the author of, among other things, *The Demands of Art* (London 1968), demonstrates uses of evaluative criticism in his account of Picasso's 'Guernica' it is an example with few repercussions. We lack a strongly developed tradition of journalistic criticism, or at least one which imposes any demands on its readership; usually it amounts to little more than free advertising, from the short notices given to commercial exhibitions to the longer explanatory accounts of the major educational shows. Only the annual show at the Royal Academy draws consistently unsympathetic reviews, perhaps because of its consistent success as a picture mart. It seems that there is a tacit recognition of the basic frailty of the art scene where all news has to be good news. Perhaps the critics are conscious of the difficulties and see their task as that of intermediaries explaining new mysteries to a bemused audience. They are less the servants of the market which they were in the nineteenth century, but now they are constrained in their judgements by what really amounts to a lack of confidence in art. The very language in which art is commonly discussed is revealing of a lack of confidence; it is felt that there is a public duty to support it as though its nature was that of an invalid constantly tottering on the brink of total collapse, and the anaemic helpfulness of criticism is no more than another expression of this fear. The inevitable result is the lack of a public debate of any quality.

The consequence of this lack of a public language not

only deprives us of the means of making an intelligent approach to painting and sculpture but results in their being placed in an absurdly defensive position, both injurious and unwarranted. Artists and their supporters are scared and this has been very apparent recently in the agitation against the absorption of art colleges into the polytechnics. Artists, it is felt, will be disregarded or persecuted by unsympathetic scientists or technologists. This intuition of a lack of sympathy may be well founded but the appearance of this trepidation in the face of potential indifference is alarming. Ideally this absorption into the polytechnic system should provide an enormously extended forum, bringing art to the attention of a group of people who ought to give it their most acute attention. It seems that quite as much as anyone else artists have been infected by the popular view that their activities are artificially sustained and that they themselves are subsidized parasites. On the contrary, it is more accurate to say that our self-esteem depends to a large degree on the presence of the artist's disinterested activity in a society dominated by commercial self-interest. Public patronage of the arts is just one of the screens which conceal from us the fundamental banalities of our capitalist society, which recognizes an ideological need for artists without being able to make proper use of them.

In some measure artists have it within their own hands to stimulate a popular understanding of their work. It is important to promote a common language of discussion, a technically based language evolved from the artist's own description and evaluation of his works. The means to promote and publicize such a discussion are available; they merely have to be recognized. Artists continue to think in terms of a division of labour in which their work is discussed and evaluated purely from the outside, by critics, in fact. This takes place, but it is wrong to assume that anything much depends on it. Formerly, of course, it was different when critics possessed immense power to shape taste and to ensure the purchase of works of art by wealthy patrons. But, where the artist's livelihood once depended on bourgeois and critical acceptance it now depends almost exclusively on the opinion of fellow artists, at every level, that is, except that of the most ambitious high art. The critic may sustain a general level of public interest but it depends on artists to decide who shall enter their profession. To attain this status entails passage through four clearly defined stages, through foundation studies onto a diploma course, from there into a post-graduate department and thence into a part-time teaching post. At each stage acceptance or rejection is in the hands of a group of artists; if the aspirant is successful at each stage he can become an artist with an established income from teaching without ever having subjected his work to criticism from the outside. To become an artist means to opt for a system almost exclusively based on progress through co-option. These are jealously guarded rights.

Yet from the point of view of establishing any general understanding of the visual arts this process has one major drawback: it reinforces the prevailing tendency towards a closed society of artists. They are probably wise to rely on their intuitions, but ought to find some way of converting these into measures which are generally understandable and publicly explained. This is crucial, for instance, at the time of the Diploma assessment when the progress of three years is surveyed and a student's work might be examined by five or six different artists, all using radically different standards of assessment. Their evaluations are finally converted into numerical grades which serve only to obscure the bases on which the work was evaluated. This is an unsatisfactory system borrowed from totally dissimilar academic areas: it easily appears to the participants as a charade put on in the interests of administrative neatness, hypocritically contrived in the interests of public relations. Of course clearly identifiable standards have been applied in the assessment: these should be made generally known both to demonstrate to the student that his work has been given serious attention, and also because this is one of the major opportunities open to artists to formulate standards and to explain them publicly. A relatively minor change of policy such as this could well have substantial ramifications for artists themselves if, in removing the quite inappropriate device of the percentage assessment, it encouraged them to give more attention to what they said and thought about art. In practical terms, then, the graded judgement should take the form of a long report on the student's work and this should be given priority. This is an obvious means of establishing a critical debate at a point where it would be of most benefit. It is the existence of such a critical debate which is the essential precondition for an understanding of art at school level: unless the all-important colleges of art set the example it is unlikely that their graduates will be able to carry on the practice throughout secondary education.

Even were it possible to establish teaching institutions with a developed awareness of a coherent theory of art, equivalent places to the Bauhaus with its careful attention to the explanation of teaching programmes, their influence might still remain slight. The visual arts in Britain have traditionally been carried out in the face of considerable public indifference. Writing in 1889, at a time when art was well patronized in Britain, the revered and successful painter G. F. Watts, RA, could claim in an essay on *The National Position of Art* that it was 'unfortunate for the object of our special interest that neither the impulse nor the deep sense of its value are felt to have any real and natural places as constituents of our national dignity. Art is cared for as an embellishment upon which to spend money, but by no means having the national importance of the turf.' This statement could well see service today and with special relevance, for the turf is an infinitely more popular way to social legitimization for the rising bourgeoisie of their new position than is patronage of the arts. By 1968 the complaint of Bryan Robertson, then director of the Whitechapel Gallery, ran on very similar lines: 'The tragedy of the situation lies in the fact that those painters and sculptors with any radical talent cannot live from the sale of their work in England, or from its totally inadequate public use.' Instances of this complaint could be multiplied from the nineteenth century when new money went on bad art, on Leader, Long and Fildes rather than on Sickert and Steer, to the present day when it is not spent on art at all. Nevertheless, the image of a successful artist remains closely associated with sales figures, in total disregard for the fact that the profession's principal orientation is towards teaching. Only a handful of artists survive through private patronage, so few in fact as to be negligible in the total body of artists: it is time, then, that the myth of the bourgeois patron as the ideal patron should finally be recognized for the illusion it is. With this achieved artists can turn unimpeded to their more fundamental social role in education.

Reading Guide

Some of the most useful insights into British art education at present are those of Dick Field in *Change in Art Education* (RKP 1970). A fine art education in this country is usually achieved in conditions which allow full play to the student's individuality: art colleges have something of the arduous liberty advocated by the Surrealists and an introduction to this can be found in *Surrealism: Permanent Revelation* by R. Cardinal and

R. S. Short (Studio Vista 1970). Many of the problems of art education today were examined in the 1920s and the provisional answers given by the Bauhaus staff in those years remain inspirational; a useful introduction to these can be found in *The Bauhaus* by Gillian Naylor (Studio Vista 1969). Very little work has been done on the sociology of art in this country but the essay 'Intellectual Field and Creative Project' by Pierre Bourdieu in *Knowledge and Control*, ed. Michael F. D. Young (Collier-Macmillan 1971), shows how this might be approached. For an example of the creative receptivity which should be expected of an artist today see the essays in *Functions of Painting* by Fernand Leger (Thames and Hudson 1973).

7. Education, Race and Society

Charles Husband

One aspect of the cultural domination exerted over the school system is the way in which our history has been mis-represented to ordinary people. Bias in the school curriculum helps to reinforce the prejudice and sustain the discrimination deeply embedded within society as a whole. Overt racialism exists, but far more pervasive is the low expectation which adults and children have of the abilities of black and brown-skinned people. Schools fail to present an adequate perspective on human cultures and so do little to combat the crude caricatures to be found in children's books and comics. Teachers themselves are subject to the false ideas which permeate our society.

Charles Husband is a Research Fellow at the Centre for Mass Communications Research at Leicester University. He is co-author with Paul Hartmann of the recently published Racism and the Mass Media *(Davis-Poynter 1974), a report of their four-year study of the role of the media in influencing white Britons' response to coloured immigration.*

Education is a highly valued commodity in this society, and like most valuable commodites techniques have evolved to guarantee its production and direct its distribution. There exists an educational system in Britain which has evolved over centuries in response to an increasing demand for educated people who can meet the needs of developing technology and the ever more specific specialisms of employment. A particular organization of teaching expertise has developed in response to changing definitions of educational needs and hence we have primary schools set up to model and cultivate the early intellectual development of our children, these are followed by secondary schools, lower schools, etc., which are charged with imparting specific areas of knowledge and developing skills; which are themselves further built upon and elaborated in high schools and upper schools. For those pupils who succeed, in terms of the aims of this educational process, there is further education in colleges, or universities to go to. This highly organized hierarchical system has a government bureaucracy all of its own in the form of the Department of Education and Science, and its own senior administrator in the person of the Minister of Education and Science. When we consider the visibility of this institutionalized education in our daily lives – our children are required to attend school, parents are probably involved in expense for clothing or materials for children at school or college, lollipop men remind us all of the frequency of schools along any town's arterial roads, and we are constantly notified via the news media of the national expense of education – it is not surprising that we tend to think of this institutionalized education as *the* basis and form of education. It is easy to see education as something you *go to* school or college *to get*, rather than a continuous *process* which is present throughout our everyday routine, of work and leisure.

There are dangers attached to seeing education as the monopoly of the educational system. It becomes all too easy to leave education to those whose job it is – leave it to the teachers; let the professionals define the problems and solve them. One consequence of having been through the educational system is the development of an easy accept

ance of specialisms, specialists and professionals. There
are teachers who specialize in maths, those who specialize
in English. Some children excel at technical drawing and
others at a foreign language and these areas of expertise are
given special attention and become the focus of effort for
O-level and A-level. Throughout the educational system in
subject after subject there are acknowledged experts, and
students learn to respect expertise and experts.

At junior school the expert may be the teacher whose
authority is based upon the assertion that 'I know best, and
I say so'; or at university the expert may be a current
academic guru whose writings are *in vogue* and whose
authority is based in the consensus of his adherents.
Despite the varying justifications of expert status there is a
common theme throughout the educational system in that
there are always experts to whom one should refer. Not
surprisingly therefore it is easy for us all to leave education
to the experts. Our doubts about our own adequacy
coupled with our, perhaps unwilling, acceptance of their
expertise combine to defuse any criticisms one may wish to
make. It is possible to see such criticisms being dissipated
in verbal eddies at bars, over coffee, and in front of the
television. Yet dissipated they are; very seldom do the
concerns and worries of individuals, or even groups,
achieve sufficient momentum to become carried through
into action. We condemn ourselves for our lack of expertise
and specialist training and leave the professionals unchallenged to make mistakes on our behalf.

When the focus of concern is race relations in this
country then all too clearly the adequacy of the professionals' skills become dubious, and their lack of serious
commitment to the issues of education in a multi-racial
society becomes a problem in itself. In this essay we will
examine ways in which the very professionalism of some
educational specialists makes them blind to their own

failings in dealing with black children. The latent racism in our culture will be examined and its consequence for the way in which teachers as individuals, and education as a set of institutions, have defined the educational needs of a multi-racial society will also be examined. It will become apparent that in an area as important as race relations we cannot complacently permit the experts to make mistakes unchecked. Indeed it is likely that without the intervention of the concerned parent and the committed layman they may never reach an adequate definition of the problem, let alone devise realistic solutions. However, before we come to deal with these matters there are other things which are best said first.

Another serious danger which follows from seeing education as the monopoly of the educational system is that we fail to see education taking place when it occurs outside of this formal system. If we regard education as instruction in social rules, the development of skills including intellectual ones, and the acquisition of knowledge then it becomes apparent that a great deal of our education occurs outside of the institutions of schools or colleges. Parents educate their children through instruction and example; individuals learn from friends they admire, colleagues they respect; and in this age of the mass media who can say he is not influenced, knowingly or unknowingly, by the content of the mass media. The learning that takes place outside of the educational system is important in itself, but it is additionally important in that it provides the environment within which the formal system must operate. Thus in considering education in a multi-racial society if we are concerned about the current practices and future potential of schools and colleges then we must first examine the larger society within which they must function. The values and beliefs which are prevalent in society at large impinge on the ways in which teachers perceive their role and assess the adequacy of their efforts. If the society itself is based upon a culture in which racism is deeply embedded then it will be possible for the educational system to teach tolerance whilst effectively discriminating against black children without this being seen. It would be possible for the schools to teach prejudice because the teachers themselves are unable to free themselves of it, and hence fail to recognize it when it occurs in textbooks.

Let us then examine the imagery of blackness in British culture and note what it tells us about our latent attitudes toward black people. From Greek and Roman times blackness has had negative connotations. It was 'the colour of ill luck, death, condemnation, malevolence' (Hunter 1967). The imagery of blackness was further developed with the coming of Christianity in which blackness was the symbol of evil and white the symbol of holiness. Such was the development of the imagery surrounding blackness that by Shakespeare's time its negative associations were firmly rooted in the minds of Englishmen. In *Othello*, Shakespeare plays upon the expectations of evil, and lasciviousness which his audience would have of the black Othello. Desdemona's father is told that his daughter is in the 'gross clasp of a lascivious Moor' and that 'an old black ram / Is tupping your white ewe'. Othello himself is referred to as a 'barbery horse' and 'the devil'. Yet much of the play's success lay in the double-take in which the usual virtues of the white Christian are found in Othello, whilst the treachery and evil is displayed by Iago. Shakespeare reflected and exploited the racial feelings current at this time in his writing, a feeling well précis'd by the Elizabethan proverb – 'Three Moors to a Portuguese, Three Portuguese to an Englishman'.

The increased contact with Africa through the development of trading voyages in the late sixteenth century in no way allayed the negative beliefs and feelings held by

Englishmen towards those with black skins. Indeed the published accounts of such voyages, as for example Hakluyt's 1589 publication of *Principal Navigations, Voyages and Discoveries of the English Nation*, served only to reinforce these beliefs. The emergence of England's interest in slave trading in the sixteenth century produced over the next two centuries a recurrent problem in relation to the black population which grew up in Britain. In 1596 Elizabeth I complained '. . . there are of late divers blackamoores brought into these realms, of which kind there are already here to manie'. Again in the latter part of the eighteenth century there arose considerable concern over the size of the black population in England, estimated at 15,000 in 1770. The black communities were associated in eighteenth century England with crime, being a burden on the parish and simultaneously a threat to Englishmen's jobs. At this time James Long said 'We must agree with those who have declared that the public good of this kingdom requires that some restraint should be laid on the unnatural increase of blacks imported into it'. (All remarkably prophetic precedences for Britain in the 1960s.)

Britain's involvement in slavery and her investments in the colonies were accompanied by the elaboration of the beliefs regarding the inferiority of the black. Initially it was essentially biblical evidence which provided the legitimating arguments for slavery and exploitation of black races, though by the eighteenth century theological arguments had become superseded by scientific ones. Even the superficial extent to which the philanthropists had been able to counter the centuries of regarding blacks as animal-like, ignorant, and variously inferior was shown in the tremendous revival of racialism following the Indian mutiny of 1857 and the Jamaican revolt of 1865. This racialism was nurtured by the Imperial activities of Britain in the late nineteenth and early twentieth century.

To speak of race in British life, or British thought, is not to refer to some recent phenomenon which has had a particular relevance in the last decade. Racist beliefs flourished at the time of Shakespeare and have flourished, metamorphosed, even receded but never died throughout history since then. As the precedents of Elizabethan and eighteenth-century England have shown, the acceptance of a black population in this country has always been a problem. Racism has been consistently evident in Britain and in her activities overseas for centuries, not years. If we are to be concerned about education and race then we must start from an acceptance of the entrenched position of racism in our culture. People do not interpret events in a historical vacuum and educational institutions operate within a society whose structure and culture reflect vested interests and entrenched beliefs.

In Britain where discriminatory practices are widespread and racism is an element of our culture, children are taught what to expect of blacks, and tutored in ways of treating them not essentially through school lessons but through observation of everyday realities and through the ubiquitous mass media. In their comics children are provided with a world in which blacks hardly figure; but where they are present in the action it is as superstitious natives; docile, humble servants; or brute savages. On only rare occasions do they approximate in behaviour and status to the whites who are the heroes of this world, and then the blacks have superficial, secondary roles. The comics reflect a British imperial past in which the white man was the civilizing master of a world whose foreign parts were peopled by ignorant heathen peoples. As Jennie Laishley said of her study of children's comics and magazines, 'the picture given of countries like Africa or India was limited and misleading, showing them as "primitive" in a way which showed no understanding of cultural differences',

Her study produced such examples as the story of 'The fighting three' in the boys' comic *Smash*. In this story the three white main characters were 'in darkest Africa' where the local inhabitants were portrayed as ignorant and ineffective savages who were referred to as 'natives' and one of them as 'you big ape'. These 'natives' were tamed by one of the white men whom they came to worship because he resembled their idol. A different, but still highly objectionable image of Africa was provided in the serial 'Safari Hotel' which was published in *June and School Friend*. The story showed an Africa dominated by whites; for whilst whites managed the hotels it was the blacks who were the servants; and the town was dominated by whites whilst black faces predominated in the 'jungle village of Darhuzin' complete with drums, grass huts and obese village chief. In stories like these the belief in white superiority is barely disguised by the story and the expressions of contempt or paternalism are clearly visible in the white characters' actions and words; visible to be emulated by children who identify with the white heroes.

That the attitudes expressed in these comics are not an object of concern among the parent population is in itself an indication of how widely dispersed in this society is the tolerance of racist and paternalist attitudes towards blacks. Nor is it only in comics that such insulting and defamatory images are transmitted; children's popular fiction too contains its share of racist assumptions. Following a survey of books for children in print in January 1970, Janet Hill came to the conclusion that 'books remain in print and continue to be published which contain not only errors of fact and biased opinions but reflect built-in attitudes of superiority and condescension . . .' This survey also produced the conclusion that many books are 'blatantly biased and prejudiced' and that 'not surprisingly this criticism applies most strongly to books about countries that have been closely connected with England, notably India, Pakistan, and the African countries'. An example of the sort of attitude that exists in these books is found in the popular W. E. Johns' Biggles series. In *Biggles and the Black Raider* our hero says he will accept a job 'on the understanding that there's no interference by bureaucrats. I want no bleating in the House of Commons about a poor innocent native being shot . . . Nobody says a word if fifty British Tommies are bumped off; but let one poor benighted heathen get the works and the balloon goes up.' It would be dangerous to assume that such material as this occurs only in very few instances. Janet Hill found that twenty-five per cent of books dealing with Africa that were surveyed were 'not recommended because their negative characteristics, whether bias, prejudice, inaccuracy or dullness, outweigh all other considerations'. There are books which provide the young readers with valid insights into life in other countries, but so much of the available fiction provides an image of Africa and Asia as being almost totally backward, and undifferentiated. The considerable variation in life-styles and people within these continents is neglected because the 'natives' are merely a back-drop to the activities of the white hero. It is the fact that the attitudes and ignorance which is sustained by these books is so consistent with existing widely held prejudice in this country that makes them doubly dangerous. Not only do they fail to destroy our ignorance of ex-colonial countries but the attitudes that they transmit are entirely consistent with those which the children can hear in the conversation of adults and friends; each source reinforces the other.

If we should be concerned about the racial attitudes to which children are exposed in reading comics or fiction, then we should certainly be highly critical of the sort of education for a multi-racial society that children obtain from television entertainment; considering the much

greater exposure they have to television. In dramatic programmes the most noticeable thing about non-whites is
their concentration in minor roles and their use in background parts where their existence is often only justifiable
as a sort of human stage setting. Blacks are predominantly
cast in subservient roles as servants, secretaries or bus
conductors and in this way the world of television entertainment reinforces the social reality. In British society blacks
visibly do occupy a large number of dirty undesirable jobs.
This fact lends credence to the widespread belief in black
inferiority in this society; blacks are believed to be inferior
on racial grounds, and their manifest occupational inferiority helps to justify this belief. The roles allotted to
blacks in television drama further reinforce this expectation
of black low status. Of course the alternative of presenting
blacks in a wide range of occupations, which included
showing them in positions of power, might well stretch the
audiences' credulity. To this extent real changes in the
dramatic presentation of blacks must be accompanied by a
radical change in their position within this society itself.

Of course a large segment of the television viewing of
children is committed to watching films in which present-
day Britain plays no part. Unfortunately this does not
mean that the content of these films are therefore irrelevant
to our concern regarding their influence on our children.
Many of the British films present accounts of history which
are flagrantly biased, and at the same time provide vivid
examples of colonial attitudes which are all too relevant to
the climate of opinion in Britain today. So often in Africa
or India the forces of Imperial Britain have been pictured
defending themselves against furious onslaughts from
frenzied natives, and the tension is usually resolved in victory for the heroic British. The historical reality behind
these scenes is a splendid irrelevance to the film industry
and thus we have the Indian sepoys who fought with the

British described as 'loyal' whilst those Indians who fought to remove British rule are described as 'traitors'. In Africa the natives are often portrayed as ignorant savages who attack the intrepid explorer, and it is a token of our national pride and closed-mindedness that it is the explorer with whom our sympathy lies. More than this it is the soldiers and the explorers who are presented as being moral and justified. The realities of British military acquisition and cultural domination are seldom reflected in these films. The old myths of Britain taking civilization to primitive societies is sustained by the imagery of barbarism and squalor that frequently forms the setting for films set in Africa and India. The great variety of cultural forms in Africa and India are largely ignored; neither the artistic skills nor the intricate social systems receive any consideration. Nor does the film industry reflect upon, for example, the barbarity of Britain's slaving activities, the visciousness of the reprisals taken for the Jamaican rebellion and Indian mutiny, or the callous and lethal inhumanity of the British concentration camps in the Boer War (in which women and children died). In the bulk of films which children can see on television Britain's imperial history of domination and exploitation exists only as an exotic setting in which wholly admirable heroes can pursue their individual destiny. The internal timespan of the story atomizes history so that our concern is one brief period of time, usually only days, wherein it is the actions of individuals that occupy our attention. Nor is it only a biased view of history that is presented in films; prejudiced attitudes are too frequently expressed in a context in which they are unobjectionable. For example, in films set in Africa it is not unusual to find expressions of disgust at the ignorance or filth of 'the natives'; their laziness, slyness, violent nature, and promiscuity all are commented upon. The objectionable aspect of these comments is that they seldom are applied to individuals, they are categorical statements made about 'natives', Negroes or Indians. Negative characteristics are imputed to whole groups of people and racial stereotypes are thus promoted. Such attitudes are not only promoted through the verbal comments of white characters for sometimes exactly the same impact is achieved through the dramatic behaviour of the natives. For example, on how many occasions has the fearless white pressed on through 'taboo' territory leaving quaking native guides and bearers gibbering in the distance. Such stereotypical portrayal of Africans is all too aceptable to a British audience who find such behaviour totally credible.

It may seem excessively nit-picking to have devoted so much time to discussing children's leisure time entertainment media, from comics to television, in terms of their educational impact. But it is precisely the fact that children do not regard comics or television plays and films as educational which make them so important. Information is acquired and attitudes modified or reinforced in a situation in which the child has his defences down. He does not assess the *validity* of actions or statements, it is only their *credibility* which is relevant in the context of enjoying the programme. Thus, in a non-purposive manner, the child acquires fragments of information to which at a later time he probably will be unable to put a source. In this way the information is indistinguishable from information derived from more scrupulous sources and it may therefore become integrated as 'fact'. The likelihood of this happening is further increased by the fact that the type of bias found in these media is found elsewhere, in textbooks, and in parents' conversation, and is therefore more readily assimilated and retained.

The news media on the other hand are highly regarded in this country and individuals go to their newspaper or television news programme with the expectation of being *told* what is going on. The particular credibility of the news media has been demonstrated in recent research which showed the important part played by the news media in influencing adults' and children's beliefs about race relations in Britain. In a survey of children and adults from widely dispersed areas of Britain, it was found that beliefs about the state of race relations were remarkably similar throughout the country. Whether it was an area of high immigration like the West Midlands or an area where there were exceedingly few immigrants, similar descriptions of race in Britain were given; and the accent was on the number of immigrants in the country, the need to stop immigration and the perception of immigrants as a problem. When the individuals were asked for the source of their information and beliefs, it was found that there was a heavy general reliance on the news media for 'facts' about race relations. Even in widely different areas where there were differences in general emotional attitudes toward blacks, and considerable differences in employment prospects and other local conditions, individuals still appeared to be taking essentially similar 'facts' from the news media. As further evidence of the impact of the news media it was found that what people said they had learned from the news media matched very closely with what a content analysis of the press showed and had been said in the papers.

In view of this important influence of the news media, it is worth while, and disturbing, to see what the content analysis of four national dailies over the period 1963 to 1970 showed of the way in which race had been covered. The press coverage of race relations overseas presented a picture of antagonism between black and white, particularly in South Africa, Rhodesia and the United States. The main features of black/white relations overseas were injustice, oppression, violence and conflict between races. A viewpoint that was also often related in stories dealing with

affairs in Britain, where America in particular was used as
an example of what could happen here. (The survey showed
that many children in fact confused reports of racial distur-
bance in the United States with events elsewhere in
Britain.) Thus as far as coverage of overseas events went,
there was every reason for the British audience to equate
black/white relations with some expectation of hostility
and trouble.

The coverage of race related events at home did not
provide a more positive picture, for the analysis showed
that over the period the press coverage of race had focussed
on immigration, especially on keeping the blacks out, on
the relationships between white and black with an emphasis on hostility between them and discrimination against
blacks, on the legislation introduced to control immigration
and race relations in Britain, and on the views of Enoch
Powell. Only marginal coverage was given to the issues of
housing, education, employment and the image of the
black as an ordinary member of society. Importantly, over
the eight-year period coverage of these important social
resources of housing, education and employment were
given progressively less importance, whilst the significance
of the issues of immigration, race relations, hostility, legislation and the numbers of immigrants increased. Thus the
British press failed to place their emphasis upon the basic
sources of antagonism in a race relations situation; namely
the control of access to the major social resources of
housing, education and employment. Instead of providing
insights into the conflicts of interest underlying racial
tension, they reported the pseudo-problems of the numbers controversy and the tension itself. In general the news
media reported race relations in Britain within a conflict
framework in which immigration was accepted as an evil
and immigrants as a problem. They failed miserably to
report on the real sources of poor housing, poor education

F

or unemployment for which the immigrants were so vociferously blamed. Failing to challenge the assumptions of popular, and party political, debate about race relations the news media were the handmaidens of the rampant racism of the 1960s and 70s. Children who at school and home saw discrimination and verbal abuse against immigrants learnt from the news media such respectable terms as 'immigrant problem' and 'curb immigration'. They accepted these definitions readily because they were the definitions prevalent in journalism and society. The news media offered no critique of the racism implicit in these terms and there was little in the child's world to make him question them. Their education had been well advanced without any attendance at school.

In what has gone before we have seen that education in Britain, perhaps particularly where it related to the acquisition of 'facts' and attitudes regarding race relations, is far from being the preserve of the institutions of education; whether they be school or college. However, this background of assumptions and attitudes exists as a force within the educational establishment. At the simplest level it means that the staff of schools bear the limiting focus upon race that comes from a lifetime spent within this culture. For those who are overtly racist it can result in their hostility towards black children being a daily example to the white pupils who thereby have their own negative predispositions reinforced. Whilst for the black child it is a particularly vicious and cruel humiliation which serves to remind him of what the experience of many of his elders in his community has indicated; namely that as a black he is not equal and certainly not welcome. I remember the derisory fusilade of support that greeted a schoolmaster instructing a black pupil to 'get back in line, you're not in the jungle now'. The look on the boy's face was also memorable, but to the master, or his fellow pupils a matter of practised irrelevance.

This may be an extreme instance but one which represents a sizable tip of a considerable iceberg. Those teachers who are less overtly racist but still unable to divest themselves of their submerged racist assumptions are just as dangerous, and much more easily found. It is this sort of unconscious racism within British education which made it possible for ESN schools to have a disproportionate number of black pupils drafted to them. To white educationists it did not seem too unreasonable that there should be an excessive number of black children in ESN schools for there was a lower expectation of their intellectual ability. A view almost parodied by a headmaster who told me with a degree of pride how good relationships were in his multi-racial school, and then proceeded to comment upon how the natural athletism of his West Indian pupils compensated for their lesser academic abilities. His concern for his black pupils was real enough, but it was wedded to such a paternalistic viewpoint that he failed to see the injustice in *his* acceptance of their lesser academic performance, and *his* emphasis upon their athletic skills. His concern was translated into a frightening willingness to accept their apparent inferiority.

This anticipation of poor performance of black pupils in British schools acts as a buffer against the inadequacies of the education offered. As long as the child is expected to perform badly, there is no incentive to look for causes when he fails. Particularly, there is no reason to question one's own skills as a teacher, or one's own ignorance of the child's real needs. Thus, although there is now a widespread acceptance of the need to provide language tuition to those children who come to school lacking proficiency in the English language, there is not yet sufficient appreciation of the fact within the profession at large that possession of a vocabulary does not constitute expertise in the language. Children who come from different cultural backgrounds may indeed know the denotive, strictly accurate, meaning of the word but yet lack adequate awareness of the many associations that can be attached to that one word. Because of the limited provision of language teaching to non-English speaking pupils in the British educational system, many children appear dim who in reality suffer only from their brightness in having a large vocabulary, without the background of cultural experience to back it up. West Indian children suffer especially since it is accepted that they speak English coming as they do from a British colony where our long domination extended to the level of imposing our own language upon the residents. Yet their English is often not classroom English and so, like working class white pupils, they under-achieve because they have a language which is not inferior, but which is not accepted as legitimate within the white middle class domain of the classroom. For the black pupil there is, however, an additional disadvantage; because the expectations of his success are lower than that of the white pupil, his predicament is more easily overlooked.

The unthinking racial bias of educationists also allows vestigial myths of our colonial glory to be taught as part of the syllabus without embarrassment or question. Thus in very many schools textbooks are still used in history or geography which continue to present caricatured images of the lazy, happy go lucky residents of the Caribbean, or speak of Africa in terms not far removed from the denigrating nineteenth-century anthropology of the 'Dark Continent'. Because the teachers themselves have absorbed the racial bias of our culture they can so easily fail to detect the gross arrogance of much of British history. So much is this the case that, even today, Britain can still be presented not only as the 'mother of Parliaments' but more broadly as the great civilizing agency of post-Roman history. The impression given is that as we created our massive territorial empire through might of arms and the motive force of the first industrial revolution; so we took law, order and culture to the heathen and the exotic. The social trauma caused by introducing allegiance to an abstract law in societies, like Burma, where the individual's responsibility was to the community or an elder is not, however, a noticeable part of this history. Nor is the preposterous conceit involved in speaking of civilizing India or Africa an apparent cause of embarrassment. Similarly the question of who was the beneficiary of the 'order' we enforced through the destruction of existing social structures is not evident in the curriculum. For many schoolchildren the Indian Mutiny is still discussed in terms of a particularly violent 'rebellion' rather than as a justified fight for liberation from oppression. Children in this country can still leave school thinking of Africa as the Victorian Englishman's adventure playground, and be totally ignorant of the highly developed African civilizations which long preceded our colonization of the continent. More than this, they are unlikely to have been given any clear understanding of our current economic colonization of Africa. To a large extent these biases are sustained by the teachers' own ignorance of alternative ways of looking at these events, and their own incapacity to view current political realities, at home and abroad, from anything other than a deeply rooted cultural and national myopia.

The impact of the passive racism within those who staff British schools is not only passive in its effect in that as in the above examples it results in the failure to perceive injustices; it also can have an active role in that it can *teach* black pupils to under-achieve. Research in the United States has shown that when teachers have low expectations of their pupils then those pupils will tend to do badly.

Whereas when those same teachers have high expectations of pupils with similar *potential*, then those children will tend to do well. It is an ironic example of the stability of a racist society that the prevalence of racist assumptions within the teaching staff can produce in their black pupils exactly those characteristics of academic inferiority which will justify the original racist assumptions. Of course these poorer academic qualifications of a large proportion of black adolescents, coupled with the existing discrimination, will further disqualify them from jobs to which status is attached. Thus the cycle will be further reinforced since it will continue to be possible to regard blacks as inferior *because* they occupy inferior positions. This generalized prejudice will then support the discrimination which keeps even those blacks who are visibly well qualified from obtaining posts at a level suitable to their skills.

The failings of the educational system in its handling of race and preparation of children for life in multi-racial Britain are very serious and affect both white and black children. The white pupil is offered no coherent alternative to the racist beliefs and patronizing sentiments prevalent in society. Thus these children will continue to practise, or at least condone, racist discrimination into their adult life. In this their education has betrayed them for not only is racism morally noxious in its own right; it is also counter-productive to the racist himself. By directing his frustration against immigrants the racist attacks a scapegoat and fails to see the basis of his deprivation where it truly lies, in the political and economic priorities of the society itself. Poor housing is not caused by immigrants, but by a political system which fails to regard adequate housing as a mini-mum right of the individual and thereby allows 'market conditions' to dictate housing availability. Similarly blacks do not cause unemployment in a society where unemployment is a weapon in the counter-inflationary arsenal. In all these areas of deprivation, because of racism, the blacks suffer more than whites but the prevalence of racist beliefs prevents the whites from seeing their mutual exploitation. Thus racism is a powerful force for maintaining existing privilege and power in that it directs the activity of the dissatisfied white away from the political realities of power and privilege which are the root cause of his deprivations.

For the black pupil the educational system fails to provide support for his developing sense of identity. Confronted by prejudice in society, the black pupil in school faces education into a hostile culture where he is allowed no history of merit and no art forms that are regarded as equivalent to those of British high culture. The richness of his own African or Indian background is given peripheral, and often token coverage, and he is encouraged to identify with a society that refuses to accept him as an equal. For the British educational system to respond more meaningfully to the future of multi-racial Britain it must shift its emphasis from promoting tolerance, to advancing justice through education. Where justice prevails there is little need of tolerance, but in a society based on tolerance it is all too easy to tolerate the inequalities of others whilst of course having sympathy with them.

For the British educational system to promote justice would of course challenge the profession's stated commitment to a non-political stance, since race in this society is an inherently political issue. In fact this 'objectivity' of educationists is itself a myth for education is in essence political. Education proceeds with the intention of making someone a 'better citizen', 'more able to get on in society' and in doing so provides the information *suited to that goal*. Education progressively shapes the child to the acceptance of certain truths and teaches him which sources of truth are valid. Behind educational practice lies a stated or unstated ideal of the end product that is being aimed at and that end product is achieved through a selection of some alternatives and a rejection of others. Thus in Britain, where 'objectivity' requires the educationist to avoid political matters, it follows that through avoiding critical comment on matters of political significance the teacher becomes by default, if not intent, a proponent of the status quo. This mythical 'objectivity' must be seen for what it is, and the educational system must enquire honestly and critically into the basis for racism and discrimination within the political and economic power structure in Britain. Failure to deal with the realities of racism is to cocoon the racism of this society in 'tolerant' cosmetics. It is absolutely meaningless to try to improve race relations in the classroom if the black child knows that outside of the artificial vacuum of the classroom he is regarded as inferior and will be discriminated against. If the educational system is to prepare citizens for a just multi-racial Britain, *it must* concern itself with the political realities underlying racism in this society. It is a tragic error to believe that education can improve racial attitudes through correcting by instruction 'mistaken beliefs regarding race'. If within society the black community remains visibly subject and inferior then such instruction would be carried on in the face of contrary daily evidence of the inferiority of the black community. Only by challenging, and changing, the relationship of domination by the white community over the black community in Britain could an educational situation be created in which racial attitudes could improve. Equality of status is best achieved through equality of power, and power can never be questioned from within an educational system in which political realities are outlawed as topics of study because they threaten the 'objectivity' of the profession. The extent to which the educational system is prepared to demonstrate commit-

ment to the future of multi-racial Britain hinges centrally
on the degree to which they are prepared to provide an
education that is critical in its examination of the current
political system and the racism within it.

At a specific level there are several things which could be
implemented rapidly and which would at least make a
start on the necessary changes. If the education which
children receive is to change then perhaps the most efficient
action can be carried out in the provision of appropriate
training for the students at teacher training colleges and
university departments of education. A recent report has
shown all too clearly the inadequacy of the training provided students to fit them to teach in multi-racial schools.
All teachers should be taught the skills needed to teach
children with varied linguistic abilities and cultural backgrounds. Just as importantly they should be fully educated
so that western Europe is no longer their only cultural and
intellectual reference point. It is vital that those who will
teach future citizens of multi-racial Britain should not be
ignorant of the culture, literature and art of Africa and
Asia. Their training must provide a sensitization to the
cultural and intellectual myopia that has for so long pervaded British education. In this way the paternalism and
racism that can be found in current school curricula will be
erased through the action of those who teach being able to
identify such bias and exclude it. For these same reasons
those teachers who are long since qualified should be
released for in-service retraining to a much greater extent
than the current meagre numbers.

Given the right climate of support within the profession
from those in positions of authority, teachers with such
training would be equipped to introduce a new critical
honesty into their subject, whether it be art, history or social
studies; thus race relations would not be an isolated and
academically peripheral subject. Rather, in a continuous

and integrated manner pupils would acquire information about other cultures and about race in Britain in a manner which made its relevance obvious.

It should not be thought that it is only multi-racial schools which require careful provision of an education suited to a multi-racial society. This same educational innovation and effort is also vitally relevant to schools and areas totally lacking in black pupils. For, given the current distribution of differing classes and races within Britain, there is a high probability that it is children from these 'white' areas who will go on to form a major part of the next generation of teachers, administrators, and in general become the new bureaucratic and professional elites. They will be the decision makers of the future. It is therefore critically important that these children are also taught to reject the racial and colonialist myths that have for so long been part of the school curriculum. If all these goals are to be achieved then there must be a vast improvement in the efforts of teacher training institutions.

Changes in teacher training and in the curricula could be aided by deliberately changing the membership of school committees and boards of governors. In many areas black parents are only too anxious to help in their children's education and yet often school committees fail to reflect this interest. There are often provisions for co-opting people onto school committees and there is a need for the black community to be given the opportunity of advising on the education, not only of their children, but of all pupils educated within the British educational system. For, after all, the futures of all these children are inevitably intertwined.

The pervasiveness of racist beliefs and practices in British society have been noted and the particular expressions of these within the educational institutions have been discussed. It has not been an account that was gratifying to write and it ought not to be comfortable to read. Certainly it ought to have at least demonstrated that there is no room whatever for complacency. For the schools of today should be preparing citizens of tomorrow and not by recycling old falsehoods in the hope that a difficult, and for some unacceptable, present will go away. We are multi-racial, we will continue to be a multi-racial society, and now more than ever we must strive to become a just society.

Bibliography

Bolton, F., and Laishley, J., *Education for a Multiracial Britain*, Fabian Society Series 303, Fabian Society, 1972

Hartmann, P., and Husband, C., *Racism and the Mass Media*, Davis-Poynter, London 1974

Hill, J. (ed.), *Books for Children; The Homelands of Immigrants in Britain*, Institute of Race Relations, London, 1971

Hunter, G. K., 'Othello and Colour Prejudice', *The Proceedings of the British Academy*. Vol. LIII, OUP, London, 1967

Laishley, J., 'Can Comics Join the Multiracial Society', *Times Educational Supplement*, 24 November 1972

Townsend, H. E. R., *Immigrant Pupils in England: the L.E.A. response*, NFER, London 1971

Townsend, H. E. R., and Brittan, E. M., *Organization in Multiracial Schools*, NFER, London 1972

Walvin, J., *The Black Presence*, Orbach and Chambers, London 1971

Reading Guide

In choosing books which would provide an introduction to further related reading I have made it a criterion of selection that the book should be paperback and generally available.

For a detailed discussion of the development of inter-racial attitudes within a historical framework *White Over Black* by Winthrop D. Jordan (Penguin 1969) is a brilliant piece of scholarship which is also remarkably readable. It can be complemented by David Brion Davies's *The Problem of Slavery in Western Culture* (Pelican 1970) which is a detailed historical analysis of attitudes to slavery up to the end of the eighteenth century. A wide-ranging discussion of attitudes towards 'inferior races' during European imperialism can be found in *The Lords of Human Kind* by V. G. Kiernan (Pelican 1972) which documents the evolution of paternalistic and racial attitudes towards 'primitive' subjects in a variety of countries.

The economic realities behind overseas domination of 'uncivilized' lands are clearly outlined, along with the consequences for the subject people, in *How Europe Underdeveloped Africa* by Walter Rodney (Bogle-L'Ouverture Publications, London 1972). The contemporary realities can be perceived in *Neo-Colonialism in West Africa* by Samir Amin (Penguin 1973) and *The South African Connection: Western Investment in Apartheid* by Ruth First, Jonathan Steele and Christable Gurney (Penguin 1973). A further complement to Rodney's book can be found in the discussions of the cultural history of Africa by Basil Davidson in which the Western myths of African 'inferiority' are shown to be more a reflection of our ignorance: *The African Past* by Basil Davidson (Penguin 1966) and *The Africans* by Basil Davidson (Penguin 1973).

As an introduction to the race relations situation in Britain I would suggest three books all born out of the individual author's unique experience of race in Britain. From a variety of viewpoints these authors provide a powerful and involving account of race in Britain: *A Portrait of English Racism* by Ann Dummett (Penguin 1973), *Black British, White British* by Dilip Hiro (Penguin 1973) and *Because They're Black* by Derek Humphry and Gus John (Penguin 1971). A more specific area, but one which indicates the potency of racial attitudes in the functioning of this society, is the involvement of race in politics. Here again there are three interesting and useful books: *Immigration and Race in British Politics* by Paul Foot (Penguin 1965), *Enoch Powell on Immigration* by Bill Smithies and Peter Fiddick (Sphere Books 1969) and *The Rise of Enoch Powell* by Paul Foot (Penguin 1969).

There are two books which indicate the difficulties of black identity in a society dominated by white cultural values: *Black Skin White Masks* by Frantz Fanon (Paladin 1970) is a classic; *The Forsaken Lover* by Chris Searle (Penguin 1973) explores the anguish of black pupils in trying to make an alien dominant white culture allow for the development of their own black identity.

For more detailed advice on reading and access to generally unavailable material I would suggest you contact the Librarian, The Institute of Race Relations, 247–249 Pentonville Road, London, N1.

The monthly magazine *Race Today* (c/o Towards Racial Justice, 184 Kings Cross Road, London, WC1, Tel. 01–837 0041) provides information about current developments in race relations in Britain not generally available in the national news media, and from a perspective that reflects the black experience of Britain.

8. The School and the Community

Ken Worpole

Not only have ordinary working people had the national history misrepresented to them in terms of imperialism and colonialism: they have also been given a very distorted picture of their own history as working people. Noting this, Ken Worpole shows that a similar disvaluation has been present in schools' attitudes towards the creative expression of ordinary people. Where pupils' creative activity is encouraged it is often regarded simply as an exercise to be quickly discarded instead of something meaningful in its own right. The local and the personal are not often sufficiently connected with the wider world which is the subject matter of 'literature' proper.

Ken Worpole himself left school at sixteen to work on a construction site. He went to Brighton College of Education as a mature student and then spent four and a half years teaching English at a East London comprehensive school. He is now running a community publishing project with links with local Hackney schools and the Workers' Education Association.

In 1911 a Mr Tom Higdon and his wife were appointed to administer and teach in a small village school in Burston, Norfolk. It was presumably not known to the school management committee which appointed them that the couple were both ardent social reformers who had previously been very involved with the cause of agricultural workers. No sooner had the two teachers settled into the village and the school, than they began to help in re-establishing and strengthening a local branch of the National Agricultural Labourers' and Rural Workers' Union. It was not long before their extra-curricular activities in the village began to cause considerable anxiety among the members of the management committee, composed as it was mainly of local farmers. This anxiety found expression in a request from that committee to the Norfolk Education Committee in 1913 that Mrs Higdon, who was the senior teacher and in charge of the school, be removed, along with her husband, to 'a more congenial sphere'. The county authorities consequently fulfilled their duties towards the management committee by ordering the Higdons to be out of the schoolhouse by or on 1 April 1914. The day came, and the children, as usual, arrived at the school, entered the classrooms and took their seats. An account, written from contemporary sources and quoted by Reg Groves in his book *Sharpen the Sickle*, describes what happened next:

Then a girl named Violet Potter walked to the front of the class, picked up a piece of chalk and wrote in large letters on the blackboard the words: 'We will go on strike.' At that the children got to their feet and marched out of the school. All the classes, numbering some sixty children, walked out.

Many of those children never returned to that school. Instead they began to attend another school, set up and furnished by the Higdons and the local parents in the workshop of an old blind carpenter named Sandy. The Higdons received no wages; instead they were fed, clothed and sheltered in turn by the villagers. A fund was started to build a new school.

The story of the Burston School Strike quickly seized the

imaginations of people throughout the country, who could find weekly progress reports in the columns of the radical press. Trade union branches organized collections; demonstrations were organized in the village which were attended by organized train-loads of trade unionists, complete with brass bands, affirming their solidarity with the Burston initiative. In 1917 the Burston Strike School was completed, and it retained the loyalty of the local villagers for many years afterwards until by degrees the provisions of the state reasserted their constituency. The Burston School Strike entered the consciousness of the labour movement as being one of those occasions in which the compulsion of events had forced the participants to hurtle after the possibilities offered by their political imaginations – and in this particular case they had caught up and refused to drift back. And in a sense they are still there today, isolated by history, frozen in a posture, because we have forgotten them. The fact that this particular incident is without any post-war documentation suggests an arrogance on our part, an assumption that many of our present theoretical and tactical positions have not been attempted before, with, in this case, a determination and a coherence that puts to shame the very marginal projects that we are offered in the Penguin Education Specials. One hopes that as a consistent project, there will be a lot more historical work done in this field, following on from the recently published History Workshop pamphlet on *Children's Strikes in 1911* which came to most of us as very modern news indeed.

One particular connection between the events of those years and the present situation arises from a phrase used in an account of the Burston Strike in which the writer described how the local people 'welcomed to Burston two teachers who shared the hopes and aspirations of the labourers'. Very similar sentiments were expressed recently by a teacher at a conference who said that he felt that one source of optimism about the present educational situation was that in many schools now teachers were prepared to abandon their traditional roles as mediators between the demands of the employment market and the limitless potentialities of the children, and were now quite clearly identifying with 'the hopes and aspirations of the children and their parents'. This issue of the self-identity of the teacher now seems to be central to any debate on educational change, because as soon as any one part of a functionally integrated institution like the school begins to change, or re-define itself, as is increasingly happening to the role of the teacher, then every other aspect of the institution requires reappraisal. There is always a heavy price to be paid for changing sides. For if the teacher begins to move out from his historical role within the institution of the school, towards the community, then all of the assumptions which seemed to be so self-explanatory, immediately become problematic. Among the most important of the ideological constellations which will probably have to be abandoned are: a totally erroneous model of history; a dualistic theory of language and a differentiated model of culture. It seems to be these three areas of focus, interconnected though they obviously are, that together form the ideological prison within which teachers find themselves trapped. And there is no point in trying to escape until there is a realization that there is somewhere worth escaping to, or that there are new possibilities for relationships and institutions worth the risk.

Who are the children we teach? Where do they come from? In nineteenth-century textbooks they were referred to, most directly, as belonging to 'the inferior ranks of society', or, more simply, 'other human creatures'. Today, many history textbooks still share Carlyle's assumption that 'the History of the World is but the biography of great men' in which the majority of the population are rendered invisible and the whole weight of the historical process is loaded onto a few shoulders, usually those of the Kings and Queens and people like Sir Francis Drake, Sir Robert Peel, Florence Nightingale, Cecil Rhodes, Winston Churchill and a few others. As a consequence, the children in the classroom have no way to recognize themselves and their parents, and the teacher has no way of recognizing the children. The basic assumption of most history teaching – and this assumption permeates the whole school – is that children themselves are a-historical, perhaps like mushrooms which are supposed to appear and disappear without leaving a trace. This attitude is paralleled in educational research, where, to quote Nell Keddie,

Researchers in education, seeking the neutrality and objectivity of scientific enquiry, have most commonly treated the child as an a-social object (rather than subject to himself and others) whose attributes can be measured by a battery of tests to reveal his intelligence quotient, social adjustment, achievement motivation, etc.

Alternatively, one can assume that they are to be rescued from their benighted past, a process that has been going on since the Elementary Education Act of 1870, and which conveniently ignores that whole, and fortunately quite well documented period of working class self-organization and self-education that preceded Mr Forster's 'progressive' Act. This latter perspective on history is characterized by those sets of history books which are supposed to be followed year by year in which Book 1 usually goes from Stone-Age Man to the Norman Conquest, Book 2 goes up to Elizabeth I, Book 3 covers the period up to 1832, Book 4 up to 1914 and Book 5 up to 1945. These series usually have breathless titles like, 'Journey Through Time' or 'The Long Journey', and if they don't employ the metaphor of a journey in the title then it is consistently there in the prose, with the assumption, of course, that by 1945 with the advent of the Welfare State we had arrived – at the end of history. Marx had noticed this perspective when he once described the bourgeois attitude as being: 'Thus there has been history, but there is no longer any.' In practice most children drop the subject, or leave, before they begin to study the post-industrial revolution period, which for them is very much the historical culture within which they and their families were formed. Schools thus bear a heavy responsibility for assisting in creating, in Adorno's terrifying description, 'The spectre of mankind without memory . . . progressing bourgeois society itself liquidates, as an irrational remnant, the faculties of recollection, time and memory.' And if the school refuses to acknowledge the history of the community within which it is set, then it is implying to the children within it that their lives are accidental, that they have come from nowhere and have, ultimately, nowhere to go.

Similarly, schools not only abstract children from historical time, but within the internal organization of the school, particularly at secondary level, they serve to destroy a natural relationship between time and work, by giving priority to a highly compartmentalized time-table and little or no priority to the requirements of the work in hand. The move from the task-oriented time of the nursery or infant class to the timed labour of the secondary school faithfully echoes the same historical pattern from that task-oriented community to the timed labour world of modern industrial capitalism. As George Lukacs puts it:

Thus time sheds its qualitative variable, flowing nature; it freezes into an exactly delimited, quantifiable continuum filled with quantifiable 'things' (the reified, mechanically objectified 'performance' of the worker, wholly separated from his total human personality): in short, it becomes space.

Lukacs' description quite clearly describes the effects of the modern secondary school organization, although he was in fact referring to the large-scale division of labour of capitalist economic life. Schools certainly do prepare children for life, although not quite in the way we hope or imagine.

We can't be sure that the a-historical nature of the modern urban community is a particularly modern phenomenon, although with the weakening of the oral tradition (which is perhaps only another half-truth) there are grounds for suspecting that certain kinds of continuities have fragmented, perhaps by the assumption – very much a part of the school tradition – that history is only to be found in textbooks. A different kind of awareness comes from that marvellous biography of a village labourer who stayed within a very small community to become its own narrator and historian, *Joseph Ashby of Tysoe*, a key book for history teaching:

But Joseph was interested now in the district he was seeing. Three things came to him in this period; some idea of how events elsewhere affected his home and village; some knowledge that other communities produced other manners and other men; and the sense, to describe it as best I can, that under the wide acreage of grass and corn and woods which he saw daily there was a ghostly, ancient tessellated pavement made of the events and thoughts and associations of other times. This historical sense he shared with many of the men he met about his work. Their strong memory for the past was unimpaired by much reading or novelty of experience, and yet their interest had been sharpened by the sense of rapid change.

This very precise description of what had happened to one particular man should also be able to stand, without any alteration, for the kind of awareness modern history work in schools should be producing: it would be very difficult to find a better model. In Joseph Ashby's case, the 'histori-

cal sense' was wholly based on spoken accounts of past
events, as each generation passed on to the next its own
version of the past, unmediated by the written word.
There is no sense in wanting to go back to a pre-literate
society in order just to preserve some of the human advantages of the exclusively oral community; on the other hand,
there is no reason why we should totally ignore the oral
history of the community – which happens in the majority
of schools – preferring to rely on the distorted generalities
of most textbooks. Just beyond any pair of school gates,
there are many people whose own personal awareness of
history may go back one hundred and twenty years,
perhaps, and who can bring the process alive by providing
the living experience of historical change. An example of
how this could be done is to look at the work of the
Workers' Educational Association in Hackney, which for
the past year has been running a course called 'A People's
Autobiography of Hackney'. The main intention of the
course was to collect the reminiscences of elderly people in
the borough in order to build up a collective picture of the
past: a collective autobiography in fact. In one year over
forty hours of tape have been collected, some of the tapes
constituting whole autobiographies themselves, in which
local people have re-told their lives, have made sense of the
sense history has made of them, to borrow Sartre's com-
pelling description.

The tapes include the reminiscences of a seventy-three-
year-old ex-seaman and music hall artist, which taken
together constitute something like fifteen hours of narrative, with not a sentence wasted, and which include an
account of local school children's strikes in 1911 (actually
part of a national phenomenon), stories of near mutinies
on merchant ships trading in the Baltic, detailed descriptions of dockside life in East London and of the problems
of the East European immigrants, of whom his own

parents were very early settlers, accounts of life on the road with the fairgrounds and later on, stories of the music hall. There is a three-hour tape made by a local shoe maker who starts his narrative by describing the small cottage industry of shoe making in which his grandfather worked and from whom his own father learned the trade (one of Hackney's traditional industries), and he goes on to discuss the whole tendency of industrialization and the move into factories in which he quite quickly found himself. In the concrete detail of this last tape, a whole economic and political process is described in an intelligible and human way, sometimes anecdotally, sometimes reflectively, that makes sense where the economic history books fail to do precisely that, other than in strictly statistical terms. There are tapes from seamen, cabinet makers, housewives, secretaries and a man who is still officially on the run having refused conscription at the start of the First World War. School children have taken part in the recording of some of these tapes and hopefully will be allowed to use some of the transcripts when they are published locally. The local autobiography offers the children, and ourselves, a mediation between the determinations within the historical process and the individual and collective struggle for autonomy and self-realization. Some extracts from the transcripts may give some indication of the quality of the experience offered:

If you were ill you were expected to go to school and if a boy was away, the teacher or the headmaster would send another boy round to his house to see why the boy hadn't come, and if he was ill to try to persuade the parents to let the boy come. He needn't do any lessons, he'd just sit in front of the class, but it was imperative that he came. In winter months, practically every day there would be five, six, seven or eight children all sitting round the fire, their heads resting on their arms and their arms resting on the fireguards. The children should either have been in bed, or, possibly, in hospital. But the thing was that they were present! And that was all-important. . . .

I would often argue with the teachers over politics. Even at that age I had a fair knowledge of politics – I was about nine I suppose at this time. I used to go to Victoria Park every Sunday on the huge piece of ground allocated for the purpose of people holding public meetings and I used to listen to the various speakers there. There were all kinds of brands of religious thought, and politically, they were mainly left wing and for my age I learned quite a lot from attending those meetings.

Albert Cullington

When I was fourteen in 1904 and left school my headmaster gave me a letter to a couple of firms who had apprenticeship schemes. And of course in those days there were no labour exchanges; decent employers always used to ask the headmasters to send along their brighter boys for apprenticeships. One I remember was a Mr Sparrow who turned out to be a sculptor who wanted a boy who was clever at drawing and of course I took along some samples of my work and he was quite satisfied with me. He said to me, 'You're a very small boy, aren't you? I shall have to give you some boxes to stand on, won't I?' I said, 'Yes, Sir, does it make any difference?' He said, 'Oh, no.' 'Because, after all,' I said, 'Nelson was a small man and look where they put him in Trafalgar Square.'

Anyway, he wanted twenty pounds premium for a seven year apprenticeship during which time I would receive half a crown a week pocket money and an extra half a crown each year until I had finished my apprenticeship as a sculptor at the age of twenty-one. And of course I went home and told my Dad that I'd got a job and he said, 'Yes, well, how much is he paying you?' I said, 'Half a crown a week.' And he said, 'Well he can stuff that for a start.' My father had a shock. He said, 'Twenty pounds! You know bloody well I haven't got twenty shillings! I had to go out to work when I was thirteen so there's no reason why you shouldn't go out to work when you're fourteen.' These jobs, of course, were impossible for the many bright boys who were then being turned out of the elementary schools who just had to become in their ultimate, errand boys, van boys, so that when they were fifteen or sixteen they were sacked and another batch of fourteen-year-olds were given their jobs.

Walter Southgate

For myself, I think the unemployment between the wars depressed me quite a bit. Mind you, there was plenty far worse off than me, but it depressed you. There's nothing like it – especially in the periods when I was out, properly out of work, perhaps six or eight months. You become demoralised; you – well you don't know what to think – you want employment but you can't get it, so you just become miserable. As a matter of fact I'd say that this sort of thing really caused me more unhappiness than anything. It was at a time when I should have been happiest of all, when you're first married, that sort of thing, and there just wasn't the opportunity, because this thing was always behind you . . . And this went on. There was obviously sheer spite from some employers towards their work-people. They seemed to glory in – well – kicking a man when he's down. I remember on one occasion, it's hardly believable but it's true, my oldest daughter – unfortunately she's not with us now, but at the time she was nearly five. This was in 1932, Christmas 1932. She was taken ill with mastoid trouble. Now in those days a mastoid operation was really serious, because they didn't know much about it, you know. Anyway she had to be operated on; it was either that or waiting for meningitis, which was inevitable. So – I think it was a Friday – we took her to the Metropolitan Hospital and during the night they operated on her. And the Friday afternoon I didn't go to work because we was taking her to hospital. I came home from work to my dinner and my wife said that she had to go to the hospital and so I went with her and I didn't go to work that afternoon. So when I went to work on the Monday she was critically ill – in fact they told us: 'You mustn't make any ideas under about five days or a week as to what is going to happen.' On the Monday morning when I went in I explained why I wasn't in on Friday afternoon. There was a nasty sort of atmosphere even under those conditions, you know. And we had no work to do, so I was just sitting down waiting for it, not being paid of course. And at ten o'clock I thought to myself, 'Well seeing as I've got nothing to do I'll go

to the Metropolitan Hospital and see or find out how she is.'
As I walked out the shop I was tackled by the one in charge and
there was just one big row because I was leaving off work that
I didn't have in order to go and see my daughter in hospital.

The street scene seems to have altered considerably since
then. The children naturally played in the streets, there wasn't
so much traffic. And the weather of course controlled the presence of people in the street, but by and large one could usually
find someone to have a short chat to. Take Sundays, then. You
were possibly disturbed from your Sunday morning 'lay-in' by
the strains of the Salvation Army band from the Citadel in Mare
Street. That was about 8.30 a.m. And after breakfast the children
would be on their way to Sunday school. And of course they
made a little noise – they were always talking and jabbering. And
soon after that the Boys' Brigade or the Scouts would come
blasting their way round the streets and again with the children
following, and the dogs would bark their disapproval. Then
there was the shrimp man, the muffin man with his tray on his
head and the ringing of a handbell. And come two-thirty the pubs
would shut for a while and then the male members of the house
next door would return home either singing or arguing politics with
the effect of the drink to egg them on. Then after dinner, the local
nuts would fly around the neighbourhood on their new-fangled
motor-bikes. This was what you call a quiet Sunday years ago.

Mr Newton

There's a feeling in a factory, that, I've often told my daughter.
I've never found the friendship anywhere like you find in a factory. They'll help you. And I remember, during the First World
War, we had to take sandwiches for our midday feed – butter,
margerine, everything like that was on ration – and one day I
went in and I told the girls that I'd got dry bread, Mother had
no margerine or butter, and they said, 'You give me one of your
dry bread slices and we'll give you a buttered slice and we'll get
over it this way.' And we did it!

Mary Philo

The use of such an approach to history – which shouldn't
of course be an exclusive approach – has many values. It

can reconnect the generations so that there is once again a realization of a shared situation, of common experiences, of the 'historical sense', remembering that it is largely the schools which have isolated the children from everybody else in the community and thus contributed to the present preoccupation with the peer group. The act of talking together may also strengthen the quality of the spoken language and help diminish the crisis which Charles Parker, for instance, writes about so urgently in *Towards a Peoples Culture*.

Such an approach to history will be strengthened by the recent revival of interest in, and subsequent publication of, working class autobiographies, as well as the tendency for more historical work to be studied at a local level and with greater emphasis on the majority experience. There are of course the excellent History Workshop pamphlets published by Ruskin College and which deal with very specific and usually highly localized topics: *A Glossary of Railwaymen's Talk*; *St Giles's Fair, 1830–1914*; *The Class Struggle in 19th century Oxfordshire*; *The Journeymen Coopers of East London*; *Club Life and Socialism in mid-Victorian London*; *Pit Life in County Durham*; *From Self Help to Glamour, the Working Men's Club 1860–1970*; *Whitsun in 19th century Oxfordshire*; *Children's Strikes in 1911*; *Pit Talk in County Durham*; *Country Girls in 19th century England*; *Big Mother and Little Mother in Matebeleland*. Obviously it is important to use these pamphlets sensibly, but they provide excellent models for the kinds of original research that could begin from schools (and, of course, any other kind of local education institution) and which would make an important contribution to the strengthening of the historical sense. Similarly, some of the most penetrating autobiographies of the last ten years, if used carefully, can really involve children with the history of others' lives and enable them to see pressures and counter-pressures, often very similar to their own, at work, and allow them to see ways of coming to terms with them, frequently by determined resistance. As such, most of them go far deeper into questions of social life than the abstract empiricism of many social studies and civic programmes. No teacher can afford not to have read Valerie Avery's *London Morning*, the autobiography of a sixteen-year-old South London girl who failed the eleven plus, but manages to describe a whole era of London working class life (1945–60) with a percipience that makes most community sociology treatises appear quite insubstantial; and Richard Pooley's *The Evacuee*, an account of how sheer economic necessity forced a young boy into theft and a subsequent twenty years spent mostly inside prison. Others that begin to sketch out the lines for a fuller picture include: A. S. Jaspar, *A Hoxton Childhood*; Grace Foakes, *Between High Walls*; Dick Fagan, *Men of the Tideway*; Jack Dash, *Good Morning, Brothers*; Valerie Avery, *London Morning*; May Hobbes, *Born to Struggle*; Ted Willis, *Whatever Happened to Tom Mix*; Bernard Kops, *The World is a Wedding*; Arthur Hopcraft, *The Great Apple Raid*; Arthur Barton, *The Penny World*; Robert Roberts, *The Classic Slum*; Spike Mays, *Reuben's Corner*; Anne Tibble, *Greenhorn*; Gordon Boswell, *The Book of Boswell*; Michael X, *From Michael de Freitas to Michael X*. This is a very incomplete list, no doubt, yet all of these books are accessible to young people and can confirm to them that the ordinary life does possess a significance, not attributed by the distorting mirror of bourgeois history.

A similar kind of process is now possible in the teaching of English. For too long the practice of English teaching has been a kind of confidence trick, in which the basic questions are never asked. Of course children should be able to read and write, but English teaching has usually seen these as strictly functional skills, so that what is read and what is written is essentially of no importance or wider significance. There is really no need here to describe the sheer gratuitousness of most elementary reading schemes and the inconsequential nature of the oral and written language work. Not surprisingly, many children fail to become motivated in any way to acquire the skills that obviously are important. Expressive writing has still not found an adequate justification apart from much spurious psychologizing about it enabling the children to come to terms with their own individual psychological history. Of course there is an important function that writing can serve in terms of enabling the child to identify, clarify and reflect on certain determinations within himself, and this function writing shares with all creative labour, yet what happens to all those pieces of paper on which are elaborated many of the children's sincerest hopes, optimistic fantasies, realistic dramatizations? In most cases, precisely nothing happens, other than that they get marked and returned, or put into an examination folder, or casually put into the waste paper basket at the end of term. If we really did acknowledge the significance of our pupils' lives, then we would do something more with their writing than hand it back with a pat on the shoulder. We cannot expect most children to carry on writing with any degree of sincerity if they see no purpose to it. Most of us do not write unless we anticipate an audience, yet we expect the children to do so. This perhaps echoes the assumptions behind the dualistic linguistic theory which is currently in the centre of English teaching philosophy: that there is something qualitatively different between 'our' language or writing and 'theirs'.

A symptomatic complaint in English teaching is that the children cannot see why reading and writing are good things in themselves, and want to know what purpose the

English work serves. This conflict does illustrate a significant difference of attitude, but it really is a superficial
antagonism, which can be resolved, perhaps not in theory
but in practice, because teachers objectively have much
more in common culturally with the children they teach
than with the world of late nineteenth-century aristocratic/
bourgeois culture which the sociologists insist that they
inhabit despite the fact that they actually exist in the latter
part of the twentieth century, in a mass culture. However,
the demand by the children for purpose is important,
because it relates quite clearly to the cultural context of
working class life which is essentially defined by its close-
ness to material production, a relationship which in turn
generates particular ideas about all forms of activity. For
historically, within various kinds of working class cultural
settings, reading and writing have been seen as foremost
productive and social activities, whether in the form of the
proselytizing writings of the non-conformist religious movements, or the pamphleteering and reading circles of the
nineteenth-century radical movements.

To suggest to many English teachers that writing is
another form of production and that it could be possible to
see the classroom, or the English lesson, as a workshop, is
to confront very firmly established ideas on the nature of
the literary process. Yet it is not at all difficult to see the
commercial world of textbooks and all other kinds of
teaching materials as being quite clearly just another
sector of capitalist production. Were we to remodel our
idea of the English lesson into that of a writing workshop,
and then begin to think about adding on a layout/artwork
centre and then a printing press, we might come very close
to the model upon which most children's idea of relevance
and usefulness is based. For why shouldn't the children we
teach become published authors and isn't it time that we
found an audience for their work? The issue is, then: how

does English teaching transform itself from an essentially individual and totally reflective activity into a form of cultural production for others, and how do we begin to think in terms of the English work we do as having some kind of social and cultural purpose that goes beyond the confines of the classroom walls?

What makes this situation now possible, to an extent not previously envisaged, is the accessibility of schools to the new reprographic technology, which enables the children to become potential cultural producers: published novelists, autobiographers, poets, historians, polemicists, film makers, radio and television producers. The world of art and culture has only just entered the era of mass production, which can also imply the possibilities for the democratization of the cultural process. Many teachers have fought shy of contact with technology, often regarding them with suspicion, or have seen it simply as a useful aid which enables them to do the old things more easily: multiple copies of textbook exercises or taped copy of an irrelevant television programme. It is interesting to note that although nearly all of the secondary schools in Inner London possess Video Tape Recorders and adapted television monitors for viewing, hardly any of them have cameras – the one item which transforms the equipment from being a medium for reproducing centrally produced programmes into a creative and democratic means of local production. In the same way, many radio stations have a preoccupation with the sound quality of tape that effectively denies the broadcasting of items made by amateurs, particularly those made by children, even though the standard of recording is quite high enough to be accessible to all but the near deaf. The case is, though, that the new media technology is potentially much more amenable to local and individual control than older methods of communication, despite its use of the means of mass production.

We now possess the technological potential to completely abolish the traditional distinction between writers and readers (producers and consumers) providing we are prepared to revise our traditional beliefs about literary production. I have described elsewhere what can happen in schools once the children's writing is taken seriously, and how this has worked out in practice. Briefly, though, in one school's English Department, quite a large section of the stock cupboard was taken up with short novels, class anthologies, and various other kinds of written work, which had been written by children within the school, cheaply printed, sometimes with photographs and line drawings, and used as teaching material with other children. With better co-ordination it will be possible to link schools within a particular area so that internally produced publications can receive a wider distribution which will in turn make possible more sophisticated printing methods. The majority of this material is far superior in quality to much of the commercially produced material, and certainly more in touch with the feelings of the children, who often have far more vivid and exciting imaginations than are catered for by the pedestrian narratives of the commercial world.

On a slightly more ambitious scale, the Centreprise Community Publishing Project, formed from the activities of individual teachers in Hackney with sponsorship from a local community centre, does offer a model of decentralized, democratic publishing that could well be taken up elsewhere. To date it has only worked on a voluntary basis, yet it has produced some impressive publications. The first project was a community based reading book, *Hackney Half Term Adventure*, entirely produced by two teachers from Hackney using local children as the characters. This reading book has now sold 2,600 copies in twenty-one months, mainly in Hackney, and generated enough confidence to think of producing a whole local reading scheme. Another project was a collection of social and historical documents about Hackney, including maps, photographs, extracts from local autobiographies, novels, transcripts of tapes made with older residents, called *If it wasn't for the houses in between* . . . The first edition of 750 packs sold out within two months and now, a year later, has sold 1,800, at a cheaper price than would be charged commercially and yet substantial profits, to be used on other projects, have been made. These others include: three individual collections of poems by Hackney school children, a paperback edition of *A Hoxton Childhood*, which is a short illustrated novel by a thirteen-year-old boy, and an autobiography, *When I Was a Child: A Hackney Childhood 1809–1913*. The success of all these publications, particularly within schools, has made it possible to employ someone full time to co-ordinate, and handle the production of, many more local projects.

The Centreprise Community Publishing Project has helped, and in turn been helped by, a very energetic local English teachers' group, with representatives from most secondary school English departments within the borough, who have been trying to produce a community based Mode II CSE syllabus which will include some of the publishing project's materials as set books for study. This kind of development, which could equally well take place within other subjects, history being a particularly good example, seems to be amongst the more significant advances in the theory of English teaching and should be watched with interest.

In no way are these developments meant to exclude the wider world of culture, history and politics; if that happened one would be arguing for the merely parochial, a response that is unfortunately made by many on the left, holding a highly theoretical (and reified) model of change which does not look beyond the collectivity of 'the masses', a category which presumably does not include themselves. This attitude can be seen in a review of an autobiography written in a left-wing newspaper, in which the reviewer began by stating, 'Marxists, their belief firmly rooted in the need for mass action, have a traditional distaste for the autobiography as a political weapon . . .' A letter from Sheila Rowbotham in response to this argument put forward quite a different view:

There are several assumptions here (in the original view) –

1. The idea of mass action is opposed to individual consciousness. The 'masses' do not cease to be individuals simply because the ruling class have no record of their names. . . .

2. It assumes that only individuals who have influenced major events are worthy of autobiography . . . Major figures can give a most distorted view of social and political movements. . . .

3. It has an ostrich-like attitude to personal consciousness. It is pre-psychoanalytic and completely ducks the important political question of the manner in which mass social consciousness is transmitted through the individual's experiences.

It in fact seems quite likely that because the majority of people have never been allowed an opportunity to speak, and have been considered invisible or hidden from history, that the power of common sense thought has held back the potentially liberating, critical, deeper feelings and beliefs which surface in the act of acknowledging the significance of the individual in the process of tape-recording an autobiography, or in providing a wider audience for the individual creative work that is produced in schools.

To talk, though, of building a new working class culture and replacing bourgeois culture is as nonsensical as making the community an exclusive focus in other kinds of study. The new culture that needs building, and in which process

G

schools could become a very important force, is one which integrates much of the old with the best of the new and potentially vast cultural forms that are becoming available. We should perhaps talk about the possibilities for a common culture, a concept that has a serious history behind it in this country, but which seems to have been forgotten in the past few years. It is probably Raymond Williams whose writings have been most identified with the idea of the common culture, and this tradition of thought, amongst the most significant to have been produced by the British left since the war, unfortunately seems to have been abandoned early on in the 1960s in favour of talking about an alternative culture, a culture which seemed to preclude anybody over thirty years of age, and most of those in traditional working class occupations. Fortunately, the possibilities for reasserting the common culture debate are now much greater with the rapid disintegration of the idealist illusions of those who advocate the alternative society. The current areas of discussion within education confirm this renewed interest in taking the debate back into the centre of the political arena, and focusing on the educational experiences of the majority of the children, typified by the beginnings of systematic work on the politics of language which Harold Rosen and others have been doing and, at a different level, Chris Searle's demand that the only hopes for radical change demand that a committed stand be taken within the state system.

Equally important are the trends within the field of 'cultural studies', developments which are quickly moving towards programmes of work which accommodate all kinds of cultural experience, in contrast to a traditional assumption that 'culture' was a very narrow field, mainly artistic, and the property of a minority. Unfortunately, much of this work is conducted and reported within a very closed world of research papers, small-run poorly distributed pamphlets and inaccessible academic publications. An example of this problem is that an essay which is probably of major importance to the debate which is described here, Alan Shuttleworth's *People and Culture* (and Stuart Hall's critical response to it), published in *Working Papers in Cultural Studies*, a Birmingham University publication, has hardly been heard of outside a very narrow academic circle. Shuttleworth's essay is an attempt to map out and explore some basic areas within which a very far-reaching programme of work is necessary:

The extension of the meaning of culture has a complicated history, but part of the energy behind the widening has been democratic. The argument here is not that in matters of culture the majority is always right; it is, rather, that everyone always has some right. The core of the argument is that an intellectual and imaginative life is not confined to one group in society alone – those who have been specially gifted or who have been specially trained for it. On the contrary, all human beings have such a life and all social living is informed by the intellect and imagination of its members. There is not a thinking, creating minority and then an inert, mechanical, working mass. Instead, there are many ways of life, each with its own centre of thought, its own characteristic ideas and images, each producing distinctive expressions, products, activities and artefacts . . .

We hold that all the thought, and all the speech and writing, actions and artefacts, of all people express interesting, worth knowing, inner life. The interpretative study (struggling into existence of all human expressions) is cultural studies. This inquiry does not only select 'good' expressions for close study: it aims to be able to study any expression. It is an interpretative study in that its main effort is to understand and then state what images and ideas, what values, what mental life those expressions embody.

There is no reason why schools should not become the centres from which such studies should begin, so that the work extends beyond the academic sphere and the com-

munity takes on the job of studying, and describing, itself.
If this happened, there would begin to emerge a much
clearer picture of the past and quite clearer possibilities for
the future. It is astonishing that a single, and quite small,
anthology of poems by older people (*Elders*, edited by
Chris Searle) should attract so much attention, as if we had
only just discovered that the older people in our society
had something to say.

All subjects in schools could be made to practically
benefit the wider community, and in fact in many schools
this is happening: older pupils (unfortunately, though, in
most cases those considered un-academic) practically help
the older people in the community; science lessons sometimes now involve the practical study of the local environment – testing pollution, making suggestions for alternative
planning schemes; secondary children go into primary
schools and playgroups to work with younger children. All
these are steps in the right direction, even though many of
them are undertaken for quite the wrong reasons and only
involve a particular proportion of the children. But the
model is there, and it is our job to critically assist this
development, to think of new ways in which what happens
in schools enlarges and strengthens the concept of community, encourages the possibilities for shared activities
and reciprocal learning. Also, since at the moment schools
possess many of the technological resources denied to the
community at large, there needs to be a move towards
making these resources more available and bringing as
many as possible local people into the schools to use them.
The question, frequently raised, as to whether the teacher
is a member of the community is simply a matter of choice
on the part of the teacher. However, it is a choice that
demands quite a high level of commitment, and the answer
depends on the individual's response to the possibilities
offered by the idea of a common culture, a practice, per-

haps the only practice, that poses a threat to the bleak, mercenary world of modern capitalism. If we can help build that culture, in whichever place we find ourselves, we will have reconnected our present situation to that of the early pioneers, and brought back the teachers, parents and children of Burston into history, as part of a continuing and progressive struggle for freedom and self-realization through the educational process.

Reading Guide

The Making of the English Working Class by E. P. Thompson (Gollancz 1963, Penguin 1968). An essential book for getting the right historical framework from which to make a positive revaluation of history teaching.

Ruskin History Workshop Pamphlets. This is a continuing series of pamphlets, mainly written by trade unionist students at Ruskin College, about detailed aspects of specific working class cultures.

What is Literature? by Jean-Paul Sartre (Methuen 1950). Many original and pertinent ideas concerning the nature of writing and the question of authorship and purpose.

The Long Revolution by Raymond Williams (Chatto and Windus 1961, Penguin 1965). Important essays around the theme of cultural democracy.

Literature and Revolution by Leon Trotsky (Ann Arbour 1960). Affirmation of the importance of literature in particular, and the arts generally, in the struggle to build a new society.

Illuminations by Walter Benjamin (Cape 1970). Essays on literature and sociology. Particularly relevant to arguments about technology and democratization of culture are 'The Work of Art in an Age of Mechanical Reproduction' and 'The Author as Producer'.

This New Season by Chris Searle (Calder and Boyars 1973). A report of work in progress, teaching with a real commitment to the community whose voices are present throughout the book.

Finally, two very important essays: 'Constituents of a Theory of the Media' by Hans Magnus Enzensberger (*New Left Review*, No. 64, 1970) and 'People and Culture' by Alan Shuttleworth (*Working Papers in Cultural Studies*, University of Birmingham, Spring 1971). Shuttleworth's essay argues for a programme of cultural work that needs doing, whilst Enzensberger shows how the new media technology can be used to subvert existing cultural configurations, and enable totally new relationships and processes to be built.

9. Relationships Among Teachers

Arnold Downes

*The impression is often given that teachers, whatever their
social origins, identify with the ideas and interests of the
middle class and therefore help to ensure that those ideas
prevail in schools. Apart from failing to appreciate the real
nature of class domination such a view ignores the complex
situation among teachers themselves. Arnold Downes con-
siders the confusion and conflict which often face teachers in
their work and also looks at the union organization of
teachers.*

*Arnold Downes has taught English in further education in
this country and abroad. He has written for the radical
teachers' papers* Rank and File *and* Blackbored *and now
works in educational publishing.*

Schools are bewildering places these days. Teachers disagree among themselves about what should be recognized
as successful learning, what kind of teaching brings about
successful learning, what kinds of attitude towards society
should be encouraged, and what kind of teacher-pupil
relationship is best. Some think that successful learning
means a pupil answering the teacher's questions with just
the answer that the teacher has in mind; others that this is
merely parrotting, and that you only know the pupil has
thought out the answer for himself when he puts it in a new

way, sometimes a way you never thought of before. Some hold the view that keeping pupils at a distance and silent, listening to the teacher or copying his statements in a book is the best way to learn; while others believe that pupils are learning most when they're solving a problem for themselves, if necessary talking to each other and to the teacher freely as they do so. Some think that the teacher should use his authority to make the children do what he knows is best for them whether they like it or not, while others feel that such treatment only makes children feel rebellious and so forces the teacher to spend more time controlling the class than actually teaching, and that successful learning is much more likely to take place if the pupils' interest can be captured in a relaxed atmosphere, even if this means apparently lowering standards at first. Some believe it is a function of school to accustom pupils to doing what they're told, as a preparation for their working lives and for obeying the laws of society; others think that only a skin-deep order can be obtained in this way, and that it is more important to get them to reason out their actions for themselves, even if this means that they may sometimes come to different conclusions from those who are in authority over them.

Where the possibility of disagreement among teachers is so great, the biggest overall problem is confusion in the mind of the child, since he is being treated in different ways and told different things by a range of figures in authority during the course of a single day. The main problem is in secondary schools. Primary schools are smaller, the teachers come into more contact with one another, there is closer communication between school and home, pupils are not big enough to seem threatening to teachers, the prospect of going out into the working world is distant, subjects are not so firmly separated from one another, and most teachers agree that interest, play, creativity and enjoyment are all part of learning at this stage. Even so, there are plenty of disagreements of the kind I have described in primary schools too. But in secondary schools there is usually much more tension on each of these counts.

Perhaps these disagreements shouldn't matter. Perhaps headmasters should determine a way of teaching for their school and make sure that the teachers stick to it. But, even if desirable, this is far beyond the powers of any one person. No secondary school headmaster can prescribe in any detail how his teachers should teach, because there are so many factors involved. The first is simply time. A teaching staff of thirty spending an average of five hours a day each in contact with large groups of children gives the head-master 150 teaching hours a day to supervise; 150 units each consisting of a ceaseless string of activities, questions, answers, discussions, incidents, emergencies. Meanwhile he has to arrange timetables, see parents, be host to inspectors, county officials, researchers and others, attend meetings and organize exams. As his role is organized at present, a secondary school headmaster is inevitably forced into a superficial position regarding the actual content and manner of teaching.

Yet he is still supposed to be responsible for these things, and while he cannot exercise an effective guiding influence, his inevitably piecemeal and arbitrary dictates can easily confound the work of other teachers. Letting assemblies run over into lesson times, changing school rules without consulting other teachers, favouring some departments or classes over others in the allocation of resources, sending pupils home for having the wrong length hair or the wrong style of clothes, punishing pupils for things which other teachers might consider innocuous – in these and dozens of other ways he is in a position to alter the psychological environment in which the teacher must work, and yet he is not there in the classroom to see the results in terms of atmosphere, relationships and willingness to learn.

And of course in a secondary school there are a number of other legitimate and inevitable influences on what and how the teacher teaches, which are not likely to come into the headmaster's expertise. There is, primarily, the individual subject, or academic discipline, in which the teacher has been trained. Neither the headmaster nor most of the other teachers know exactly what goes on in any one subject and what kind of teaching it requires. Then there is the teacher's educational training. Different teachers will have absorbed different ideas and skills from their different colleges. More distant but still important are the mingling influences of county advisers, Department of Education and Science inspectors, school governors, broadcasters, journalists and publishers. Differences of approach and aim are expressed in the advice and concern of all these groups.

The Traditional Solution is Actually the Problem

The traditional way of coping with all these differences is to draw an imaginary line around each individual lesson and let the individual teacher get on with his allocation of lessons. So long as teachers do not interest themselves too closely in the state of mind of the pupils arriving in that lesson or in what is to confront them when they leave it; so long as teachers do not listen very much to what pupils have to say for themselves other than when directly answering the teacher's impersonal questions, and do not wonder what pupils are really thinking and feeling about the lesson; so long as by tacit agreement teachers do not ask each other too closely about their methods or attitudes or what they have been teaching and whether or not it seemed to be getting across, while any kind of nonconformity or disagreement by pupils can confidently be attributed to misbehaviour or lack of intelligence; so long as all these arbitrary borders are observed, it is possible to keep up an appearance of order. This is the traditional order of the school.

But traditional order is only organizational, not educational order. It is order from the point of view of a staff-room where there is no overall plan, in spite of the fact that the success of each teacher's work depends intimately on the others'. From the point of view of the child, who must pass from one subject, one teacher, one state of mind, one set of expectations and attitudes and authority styles to another, and then another and another, every three quarters of an hour at the sound of a bell, this is not order. It is utter confusion. No wonder only a minority of children appear capable of good intellectual work.

It sometimes seems that the introduction of progressive methods in schools has caused a lot of confusion, and some people have called for a return to the order of the traditional school. Certainly not all new methods are good because they are called progressive, but it is basically the confusion of *traditional* methods that has been revealed by the progressive challenge. The progressives have merely subjected traditional schooling to rational scrutiny and revealed the educational disorder. For, as soon as you try to think out rationally how children learn, the traditional barriers have to be questioned. This does not mean they must be swept away, and in practice progressive methods never mean anything as simple minded as this. Pupils need some kind of order to give them an idea of what to expect and what is expected of them, but they need an order that they can consent to and that is best designed to help them learn. Traditional order has not been based on these principles at all.

The Progressive Challenge

If you really want children to learn, you have to become interested in how learning takes place in the human mind. The first thing you have to realize – and remain sensitive to – is the existing state of mind of the pupils whom you confront. You cannot be indifferent to what they have been learning with other teachers. You cannot ignore whether different teachers are telling them contradictory things. Similarly, you begin to pay attention to home background. If you present a very different picture of the world, based on very different assumptions, from the one a pupil has grown up into, what you are saying may be unable to take root. Unless you listen to what pupils have to say for themselves, you can't pitch what *you* say at just the right level of difficulty, because you don't know which words, concepts, facts and ideas the pupil already has at his disposal and which are quite new to him.

Once you start listening to pupils carefully and extensively you discover all sorts of mistakes that were hidden before. You find that a child whom you thought stupid or disruptive was actually slightly deaf, and needed to be at the front of the class, or that a pupil whom you thought clever merely had a knack of echoing your words without grasping their meanings. You discover that pupils learn as much or more from each other as they do from you, and that what was formerly called cheating is actually one of the most effective ways in which an idea grasped from you by a few of the quicker children is spread and understood by the whole class. It becomes apparent that the whole class is not some mystic unity but has a wide range of understandings and pictures of the world and that children cannot learn solely by listening and repeating. They need to talk the new ideas over, with you and each other, in a free, exploratory way, because talking is not merely delivering ready prepared thoughts – it is a means of developing the thoughts themselves. You discover, above all, that some pupils who had seemed to be uninterested in and incapable of intellectual work were actually playing dumb and passive because their existence as people with thoughts and feelings of their own had not, until now, been acknowledged.

The Community of Teachers

Once you start trying to make your teaching rational, the implications and the necessary connections reach far beyond the individual lesson. How can you successfully encourage pupils to express their own thoughts when they have just come out of a lesson where this very thing was penalized? Is it possible to encourage pupils to take every opportunity to talk ideas over with each other when there is a rule of silence in the corridors? By what means can you persuade slower pupils that they are able to solve problems if they try, and that worlds will thereby be opened to them, if, by sarcasm, threats and discouragement, other teachers are making them feel they have no chance?

The answer to the confusion is not in going back to the situation in which confusion was concealed. It is in progressing to a situation in which it is recognized that the community of teachers must work together to create a learning environment in which contradictions are minimized and mutual support maximized. If this became established practice, the further advantages to learning would be immense. The psychological strain on the teacher would be eased: he would no longer be isolated, having to hide his failures or blame the children. The recognition of common difficulties and mutual support would enable him to feel less threatened by pupils and so relate to them more tolerantly and constructively. Democratic staff-room discussion would decide which selection of educational practices made most sense at each stage of the development of the school. There would be intellectually exciting opportunities for the content of different lessons and subjects to link up and extend each other, and so encourage the minds of pupils and teachers alike to perceive a unified world.

Assuredly, this would not solve the problem of the *pupils'* democratic participation in school life – a necessary aim without which pupils will never really be able to identify with their place of learning and therefore never be able to make optimum use of it. Nor would it solve the problem of the out of school influences which ultimately make the school what it is – the policies of the government and of local government, the demands of employers, the influence of the universities and so on. But it is the most viable short-term aim which could change the effectiveness of schools as places to make learning possible. Without the experience of democracy among themselves teachers will never have the degree of psychological security to be able to accept democratic relations between themselves and pupils. And with such democracy they would be in a far better position to confront the outside pressures too.

The kind of democracy I have in mind is not the election of one or two teachers to serve on governing bodies. This may be of some value but it is marginal to the day-to-day coherence of the school as a learning community. Relationships among the staff themselves are far more important: together they will take a stand, on whatever issues they feel to be educationally important, and periodically explain their activities to the governors or headmaster or whoever is the appropriate authority. On some issues they will not even need to do this, since agreement among themselves on issues which are normally in effect left up to the individual teacher will automatically become school policy. This democratic base could not, whatever demands it might eventually agree upon, be *achieved* by formal decree, though it would need formal *recognition* of some kind. It is likely to start by groups of allies forming themselves among teachers who seek to co-ordinate their educational aims.

The Bias Against Working Class Pupils

Aims have to do with life outside the school as well as within it, particularly with the prospects of work. Here we come to the single biggest disorder in traditional education revealed by the progressive challenge: the heavy bias against working class pupils. Working class pupils – in other words the majority of the school population – have never, on average, done as well at school as middle class pupils. For generations it was believed or pretended that this was because they were less intelligent and had less ability, but now that we know so much more about the underlying educational disorder of schools, it is easy to see that the failure of working class pupils is as much a creation and a projection of the schools as it is intrinsic. It is not *entirely* a creation of schools, as some deschooling writers appear to think, for the purely material disadvantages of many working class homes no doubt affect learning capacity just as they affect everything else; not because working class people are less intelligent or able or are culturally inferior or don't use words so well but because you cannot easily concentrate on learning if you are undernourished, harassed or exhausted. And yet schools, instead of counteracting these disadvantages, have added further disadvantages of their own.

The eleven plus exam is only the most notorious of these, disheartening five pupils for every one that it encourages. Streaming within schools compounds the bad effect.

Pupils who feel they have been labelled failures lose interest in working, seem to slip further, make the teacher's life more difficult; teachers feel threatened, are aware that the pupils aren't getting anywhere and, to shield themselves from blame and self-blame, cling to the belief that pupils are stupid. Pupils who are creative, like to think things through for themselves, are good at talking and are lively may risk the teacher's hostility and discouragement, while those who imitate the teacher's way of talking, are docile and write neatly are likely to be encouraged and get good marks. Intelligent pupils who are disheartened become resentful of school and rebellious, and get labelled as behaviour problems; teachers get nervous about them and become obsessed with control. By expecting working class pupils not to do well and treating them accordingly teachers inadvertently make it even less likely that they will try, and so the vicious circle begins again.

All this however is not the spontaneous creation of teachers. It is largely the effect of the situation into which teachers, like pupils, are plunged without quite knowing what to expect; a situation in which greater respect and resources are given to the successful few than the unsuccessful many; in which those pupils destined to take A-levels and so be set on the road to respectability get better paid teachers, more textbooks and equipment, smaller numbers in the class and more encouragement.

What is Preparation for Work?

Undoubtedly the main structuring element in schools has been the public examination system, which forms the junction of school life, working life and the academic measurement of attainment. It would be futile for schools to attempt to become self-contained systems in which no relation to the rest of society was visible. Indeed, one of the faults of the traditional school is that it has pretended to be much more independent of society than it can be, while actually dividing people up for different work destinies in the crudest manner, picking out the few for favoured treatment and leaving the others to fare as best they could.

But there are different ways in which school can orientate to the world of work, depending on its idea of what being a good worker means and of the place of paid work in life. Is good working ability simply the ability to do a given job, or is it also the ability to understand the work you have to do in the widest sense? The ability to understand the role of your particular job in society as a whole, the history, the laws, the inventions, the conditions influencing it, its relation to other jobs in society; the ability to defend your interests at your place of work, and relate democratically to those who work with you, to understand and make judgements on the social, economic and political frameworks which govern, and also reflect, the way work is organized in our society; the ability, for sanity and emotion's sake, to understand the strains that work imposes on one's personality and relationships – all these are parts of a proper understanding of preparing people for work. And there are of course many aspects of life for which pupils could beneficially be prepared which do not come under the heading of work at all.

When it has spoken of preparing working class pupils for their working life, the traditional school has had in mind the bare capacity to operate the tools and the disposition to take orders. Little thought has been given to what the right preparation would be for a world in which there was an increasing diffusion of initiative, responsibility and influence on aims among the whole working population.

Since, then, exams are the means by which the school stratifies the population for its various approximate working destinies, the debate over exams is a reflection of the feelings of society about its system of employment in general. Here we run into a major ambiguity: you may criticize exams (and the courses that lead up to them) either because you are happy about the employment system as it is but you think that schools are not preparing people for it well, *or* because you are unhappy with the employment system and you think that it and education alike would be improved if schools prepared pupils in a different way.

Both kinds of criticism may claim the title educationally progressive because they both express dissatisfaction with schools as they are, but they lead to different conclusions. When people complain of the irrelevance of traditional education for working class pupils they might mean that learning about Shakespeare and the French Revolution is irrelevant to someone who only needs to know how to handle machinery in order to survive, so why waste effort offering him wider horizons? On the other hand, they might mean that Shakespeare and the French Revolution (and many contemporary topics too) are taught in such a way that they seem to have no connection with ordinary life today, whereas they have a great deal to say to us if we know how to interpret them from our own standpoint; but, at the same time, pupils can only be expected to address themselves to such things if their minds are at rest about more immediate worries such as knowing they will be able to earn a living when the time comes.

The first kind of progressivism is in danger of not being progressive at all but of imposing as many limitations on working class pupils as the traditional school did. Into this category fall the arguments of those educationalists who say that it is no longer important for working class children to learn to read, because they can get what they need to know from television and talk, or no longer important to learn mathematics because calculating machines and computers are now accessible. People who have this sort of progress in mind tend to end up by wanting to abolish schools altogether, for they say that whatever pupils learn or fail to learn at school they can learn better from industry and the environment direct; as though education consisted solely in finding out about things as they are at this moment in the immediate locality of the individual, not in finding out what they have been at other times and in other places, nor how we got to the state we are in, nor the deeper explanations of present circumstances, nor what variety of further possibilities there may be. Behind this superficial progressivism is the idea that all that matters and need matter to the working class person is survival and keeping himself amused when he's not working. If, on the other hand, you think that survival is merely the first condition for a full life, a life in which depth of experience and quality of fulfilment matter, a life which includes influencing, as well as being influenced by, your social environment, the whole of human history and thought is your source book. In this case it is not the fact that these things are taught but the way they are taught – including the way they are interpreted – that is at fault.

If the harsh things I have said about schools and teaching are true, how can they be improved? The idea that the whole education system should be scrapped is a counsel of despair. Progressive methods that have been well thought out are demonstrating results sufficient to show that they are viable on a wider scale. Not all the obstacles to effective universal education are extrinsic to the education system, and many could be alleviated if they were understood.

There are many factors hindering the effectiveness of teaching, and one important way in which they do so is by their influence on the psychological predicament of the teacher. The training he has received at university or college, the hierarchical order or disorder of the school, and various pressures from outside the school combine to produce a psychological atmosphere which impedes rather than aids him in his job.

One particular form of impediment is the idea that school ought to be and is a preparation for work only in the narrow sense outlined above. The idea that school is primarily a means of qualifying people to do jobs seems, at first sight, to give teachers a strong hand in their dealings with pupils, since those pupils' careers are, in a sense, in the teacher's hands. In practice it frequently works in the opposite manner. If learning is just a means of qualifying for a job, then once you know you are not being groomed for a good job, a job that requires A-levels and higher education, why make an effort? Once you know you are destined for the sort of job that your dad or mum does already without needing to know anything about Shakespeare or the French Revolution, nine tenths of what school has to offer looks irrelevant. If school has not succeeded, not even tried, to convince you that what it offers will be of use and interest to you *personally*, for reasons to do with your own experiences, wishes, hopes, fears, pleasures and relationships, you can hardly be expected to convince yourself of it. If the teacher relies on the whip of discipline and the carrot of a good job, which at the same time he and you know is out of reach, in order to *make* you learn, you sense quickly enough that he is not himself convinced of the intrinsic value of learning for you – or possibly even for himself. In his own case, after all, learning has been just what he is saying it ought to be for you: a means of earning a living. If he is not convinced of its wider and deeper value to himself, he can hardly convince you of its wider and deeper value either.

Salaries and Finance

The principle of hierarchy in schools is built into the way in which education is financed. Teachers' salaries vary between £1,300 and about £6,000 a year (in July 1973), the great majority of teachers, of course, being much nearer the bottom than the top end. The differences are determined not only by seniority but by what sort of school you are in, whether you have a university degree or not, and whether you have responsibilities such as care of the school library, planning the timetable, being a headmaster, being a head of department or a housemaster. (Also, heads of large schools are paid more than heads of small schools.)

Now, important as these responsibilities are, none of them is more important or more difficult and demanding than the job of teaching itself. It is on the quality of this direct contact with pupils that the value of schooling most crucially depends. Yet career advancement involves getting further away from this direct contact and progressively substituting for it various administrative chores. The teacher who really likes teaching and wants to stay close to the pupils is liable to stay at the bottom, financially speaking. And since there are only a limited number of responsibility awards and high paid posts, a quiet, long-drawn-out rat race is in progress in many schools which again gets in the way of a frank and co-operative atmosphere among teachers.

There is a financial hierarchy between educational institutions as well as within them. Universities get much higher sums of public money for the number of students who attend them (about 5 per cent of the population) than other higher education institutions, and vastly more than schools. Within the money allocated to schools, primary get less than secondary, and secondary modern and comprehensive less than grammar schools (because certain

allowances are based on the age of pupils, and grammar
schools have a higher proportion of pupils over sixteen).
There are also considerable regional discrepancies, according to the details of policy of different Local Education
Authorities. The range of differences from school to school
in terms of stability of teachers, availability of textbooks
and equipment and extent of facilities can be marked.
Where there is a squeeze on the essential tools of the trade,
the pyramidal pattern within each school is liable to be
reinforced: scarce textbook and equipment money will go
to exam streams as a priority, and the disadvantaged
classes will get what is left.

   The teaching force in schools is made up of two types of
teacher, those with degrees and those with certificates.
Those with degrees (about a fifth of all teachers) have been
to universities and had twice as much spent on their higher
education as those with certificates, who have been to
colleges of education. Those with degrees automatically get
paid more as teachers, and their chances of getting the
posts of 'responsibility' and the exam streams to teach
(which are usually less strenuous) are greater. Although
there are exceptions and variations, it is not too much to say
that there are broadly two classes of teacher: the relatively
privileged class to teach the more privileged, exam-
oriented, predominantly middle class pupils, and the less
privileged class to teach the less privileged, educationally
discouraged, predominantly working class pupils. The jobs
of neither of these groups is easy, but the group that has the
harder job also has less reward, less influence and less
support. Here then is another feature of the school community standing in the way of the development of a democratic atmosphere.

Democracy in Schools

Democracy is important in schools for similar reasons that it is important in society as a whole: not only that the largest reconcilable number of people shall determine decisions affecting all, not only that the objections of minorities and individuals shall also have had the opportunity to change the mind of the majority and modify the decisions, but also that the reasons for decisions shall have been publicly weighed and argued and shall therefore have been absorbed by the whole community that is to abide by them. Decisions imposed from on high cannot have the same effect or obtain the same consent. Apart from the likelihood that they will be biased towards the interests of the clique who make them, they will not have been sharpened by the multi-faceted analysis which only free critical debate can provide, nor will they be surrounded by an understanding of the purpose and reasoning behind them, disseminated by that same free critical debate.

Where and when is this more true than in schools now, in the situation of deep conflicts of values and practices? Certainly some headmasters are better than others, but no single person can be, or ought to have to try to be, the all seeing, all knowing saint that a headmaster would have to be to really do his job. To put a single human being in a position of total responsibility for everything that goes on in a community of many hundreds is to put him in a situation which will make disasters of his slightest weaknesses.

A head may be progressive and attempt to institute progressive practices by his individual decision, but this approach is fraught with dangers. The changes of teaching approach, philosophy and relationships needed among the body of teachers in order to make de-streaming, team teaching or pupil centred objectives work cannot come about by decree. The staff, experiencing the problems so much more intimately than the head, will become frustrated and resentful at the lack of opportunity to shape the changes to the exact conditions prevailing. New policies carried out without conviction will fail to take, and the resulting confusion and disappointment will be as bad as before.

Lacking the experience of workplace democracy themselves, how can teachers pass on a rationale of greater autonomy to the pupils? They will not have been able to work through to a practical understanding of the interdependence of equal individuals in community, or of the value of an order based on the development of agreed rules. A shallow notion of progressivism can easily become current, because the staff have not been able to argue the proposed changes through, and on this basis the new ideas cannot work.

Lasting and fruitful changes can only be created by the people who must implement them because only thus can the changes be sufficiently internalized to command the confidence of those people and hence of those (the pupils) whom they hope to influence. Wave after wave of educational reform still comes in the self-defeating form of an imposition from above, whether by teacher trainers on students, education authorities on headmasters or headmasters on teachers.

So far from being a threat to schools, staff-room democracy, leading eventually to the development of viable forms of pupil democracy too, is the only thing that can enable them to hold together in this confused, agonized period. Schools need rules that are not arbitrary but reflect a visible rationale. The only way that rules which will be respected by all can be achieved, is by being worked out by all in the view of all. Democratic participation gives an institution an inner identity that the creators and adminis-

trators of an institution can never give to it. Before the
development of internal pressures for collective control,
the members of an institution are merely a collection of
individuals thrown together by external accident. Through
it, they acquire an identity in common.

There are a number of agencies devoted to promoting
reform in schools, and since the government funds some of
them, you could say that it supports the idea of such
reform. For example, the Department of Education and
Science helps to support the Schools Council, a body set up
in 1964 to advise the government on reform of the school
curriculum, that is, everything of educational significance
that goes on in schools. It also provides money for research
intended to discover which educational practices are most
effective. The sums involved are tiny compared to the
budget for education as a whole, but educational research
and development do act as useful stimulants on the education system, at least in accustoming people to recognize
that there are new ideas to be tried and to ask themselves
whether what they are doing in the classroom is working
or not.

However, the most effective ways in which government
could stimulate educational progress (apart from raising
minimum standards of living in general) would be to
equalize financial resources over different schools and to
equalize teachers' salaries and responsibilities. Measures
such as these are hardly even contemplated in educational
research and development. Only concerted pressure by
teachers themselves could put such changes on the agenda.

Without such a change, all efforts at educational reform, though not futile, tend to become assimilated to the
pattern of things as they are. For example, we have already
seen that headmasters are very unrepresentative of teachers
as a whole. They get salaries sometimes four or five times
as much as young teachers in the same schools, they do less

actual teaching than anyone else in the school, they are appointed as administrators rather than educators, and they have virtually dictatorial powers within their schools which are liable to alienate them from the rest of the staff. Yet wherever teachers are represented, including salary negotiations, it is predominantly headmasters who represent them. It is thus the headmasters' point of view rather than that of teachers in the classroom, which tends to come to the surface in proposals for educational reform as in everything else. Yet the very nature of the headmaster's position is such that it gets in the way of reforms which some headmasters themselves may sincerely support. The educational influence of the institution of headmasters is the most obvious and neglected aspect of schools that could be researched. But because of their position, it is the last subject that is actually likely to be researched.

The predominance of headmasters in educational politics is ensured partly by their almost unassailable position in schools and partly by their dominance in the teachers' unions. The latter fact is itself partly a reflection of the former – heads have more opportunity to engage in educational politics than other teachers, if only by having relative freedom of movement in work time, and the use of a phone, a secretary and an office at work – and partly a testimony to the lack of a tradition of democratic consciousness among teachers.

Developments in the last few years suggest that such a consciousness may now be developing, because of the increasing demands made on teachers, the emergence of education as a politically sensitive area and the changing mood in the country generally. But it is not, of course, a smooth transition, and the complicated, fragmented state of the teachers' unions at present reflects both the democratic pressures to reform and the obstacles in their way.

The Teachers' Unions

The largest teachers' union, the NUT, has about 235,000 members, and is also the most progressive in its educational policies. A pressure group within it called 'Rank and File' has for some five years been urging a policy of equalization of salaries and democratization of schools, though exactly what the latter means is in some dispute. Although the union as a whole has by no means adopted these policies it has fought for increases in the basic scale and is tentatively exploring the idea of teacher participation in the running of schools. Its strongest rival, the National Association of Schoolmasters, with about 60,000 members, has, by contrast, a reactionary if militant image. Closed to women (who form about 70 per cent of the profession), the NAS bases its philosophy on the interests of what it conceives as the career teacher – most career teachers being men. The implication is that advancement and responsibility are less important to women teachers and that this is the way it ought to be. Men do indeed occupy a disproportionate number of senior posts, but whether this is because they are any more dedicated to the job or any better at it may be doubted. Nevertheless, the NAS has a female counterpart, the Union of Women Teachers, with 14,500 members, who share some of its attitudes.

On the salaries question the NAS is far more interested in boosting differentials than in raising the basic. On educational attitudes an example of the difference between it and the NUT is that it stresses the incidence of violence in schools at the risk of being alarmist, and leans towards the idea of holding down violence with violence (the cane); the NUT, though by no means overwhelmingly against caning, has shown more awareness that reports of pupil violence are often sensationalized and that where pupils are genuinely violent it is sometimes a reaction to frustration and provocation from teachers themselves, and that heavy handed attitudes are liable to exacerbate the problem. London NUT members have even called on the local education authority to ban the cane.

There is, further, a union specifically for head teachers, the National Association of Head Teachers, with 17,000 members, although many heads are sprinkled through the other unions, and are frequently exceptionally influential in them. And, showing further the degree of fragmentation in the profession, there are another four unions, known as the 'Joint Four', who work in loose association with each other but claim to represent the distinct interests of head-masters, headmistresses, assistant masters and assistant mistresses respectively. (All teachers other than heads are technically known as assistants!) The Joint Four claim a membership of 65,000 between them. In addition, there is a union founded in 1970 and now claiming 6,000 members, the Professional Association of Teachers, whose basis is a pledge never to go on strike. This leaves something like a further 50,000 teachers who are probably in no union at all.

Teachers' unions do not have a presence in schools in the way that industrial unions do in factories. Even the largest school only has a workforce as large as that in a small factory. The fragmented union affiliations make it difficult for school staffs to act together on a union basis. The varied unions reflect differences in educational atti-tudes as well as different perceptions of members' interests.

Teachers who see pupils as a hostile group against whom they must protect their interests as much as they must against employers are likely to have fundamentally opposed educational attitudes to those who see their interests as ideally converging with those of pupils. Yet even within single unions there are wide divergences of educational opinion.

Thus a teacher struggling to implement educationally

progressive ideas within his school cannot rely on the support of his union, even if that union is the NUT, especially if he thereby finds himself in conflict with the headmaster or other teachers. For all sorts of reasons, many of which I have tried to bring out in this essay, he will be fighting, initially at any rate, a many faceted but often lonely battle.

Ultimately his best hope lies in getting across to the other teachers with whom he works, at least those who retain some element of the belief in the future which may originally have been one of their reasons for becoming teachers. If he wants the support of the union too, and it is difficult to see how educational progress could be realized on any scale if the policies of major unions ran counter to it, he is compelled to engage in a simultaneous struggle *within* the union, to strengthen its commitment to progressive educational policies. Clearly the NUT is the union most likely to be capable of playing such a role, and is already in some respects geared to it.

Conclusion: Coping and More

If this discussion has left the impression that a teacher may find himself struggling on half a dozen different fronts at once, the conclusion cannot be denied. Few jobs are as nerve racking as a teacher's. Few jobs make demands of the whole person in such a relentless way – intellectually, emotionally, tactically and socially at once. My main point has been that the educational success or failure of schools depends crucially on relationships among teachers, not merely on the abilities of the teacher as an isolated individual. It is as an isolated individual that teacher training and educational theory and research mainly view him, which is one reason why these activities frequently fail to have any decisive influence on schools.

While this complicated, strenuous situation endures, how can teachers and parents best live with it? For teachers who cannot abandon the idea that they are there to help *all* children develop to the fullest of their potential, and who therefore find themselves at odds with many aspects of the schools as they are, securing allies amongst themselves is essential for maintaining sanity, let alone for influencing progress. For parents, teachers and pupils alike, the confusion may become more manageable, mentally and tactically, once it is recognized that the functions of the school and the aims of education may at some points diverge widely, and that there is therefore likely to be a *necessary* disjunction, and a *fruitful* tension between the good teacher's efforts to educate and many other features of school life.

Finally, fighting on many fronts may be a way of achieving a sense of wholeness which cannot, in our fragmented society, be achieved in any other way. The energy and intelligence we have for social struggle (or for living in general) is not a fixed quantity. There is a certain superficial behaviourist image of human beings which conceives them as static units with fixed, measurable abilities and attributes – an image still very widespread in educational literature, and one that severely holds back educational progress. If we see human beings not in this way but as flexible, many sided, autonomous, developing, interacting social creatures, we should apply this to teachers as well as pupils. The teacher is not a finished human being who serves as a model of the standard adult or as a dispensary of accumulated, unchanging knowledge. His ability to relate to pupils as beings in a dynamic state of development depends on the sense of his own continuing development and this is vitally affected by relationships in his working situation. The cross currents, the reciprocal stimulation, which come from thinking and acting in a number of different related spheres generates more energy than it expends, and because it enables us to understand our predicament in a rounded, integrated way, it produces a far fuller understanding of any individual issue.

10. The 'Free Schoolers'

Guy Neave

Some people have argued that the state system of schools is beyond rescue, totally at the mercy of the ruling ideology and rejected by a growing number of young working class people who vote with their feet, swelling the numbers of habitual truants. The answer is seen to lie either in so-called 'de-schooling' – abolishing compulsory schools altogether – or in setting up 'free schools', organized outside the ordinary system on a voluntary basis, mainly for the children of the city centres.

While 'de-schooling' may appeal to many dissident middle class people it is hardly relevant to the main problem of social and cultural domination. 'Free schools' on the other hand are aimed, in this country at least, at the children of the most dominated people. Guy Neave seeks to demonstrate that this approach too is, in the end, equally irrelevant. He traces similar movements here and in nineteenth-century France among the anarcho-syndicalist trade unionists. Radicals, he maintains, cannot effectively challenge the manipulation of the state schools by simply opting out.

Guy Neave is a Research Fellow at the University of Edinburgh Centre for Educational Sociology. He taught Modern European History at the University College of North Wales before changing fields to undertake research into comprehensive school students at university. The results

are to be published shortly by Routledge and Kegan Paul as
The Comprehensive School and the University.

'War,' a French statesman once remarked, 'is too important to be left to generals.' The same issue is being posed
today about education, schools and teachers. Is education
too important to be left to teachers or to educational
administrators? Should education indeed be equated with
the school? Or should we seek some other form of institution outside the school? Or, alternatively, as some of the
more heretical sects in the education world are proposing,
abolish the school entirely? These are just some of the
questions that have come increasingly to the attention of
the educational world through the influence of two movements – the 'free schoolers' and the 'de-schoolers'.

Virtually unknown five years ago, these two groups have
gathered a considerable following. Several large cities –
London, Liverpool and Nottingham – have seen enthusiastic volunteers put some of their ideas into practice. As
yet, however, 'free schools' are thin on the ground. In the
main, they cater for those children who have dropped out
of the 'official school', providing part refuge, part senior
play school, an alternative to compulsory education or, as
some would point out, the educational equivalent of the
'counter culture' of the late 1960s.

Attendance at the 'free schools' is not compulsory, nor
is it full time. Small street corner Summerhills, they believe
that children will learn when they are ready to do so.
Children come and go as they wish, learn what they are
interested in at the moment. For if attendance is not compulsory then neither is there a compulsory and standard
curriculum.

To the sceptic or the cynic, the creation of 'free schools'
in downtown areas of large cities appears very much a

H

latter day edition of the Oxford University Missions to the East End of London during the 1880s – a Salvation Army with chalk and talk instead of tambourines and trombones. To others, however, the 'free school' movement comes as a stimulating challenge to one of the basic premisses on which the whole of educational reform for the past seventy years has rested: that education should take place in schools. The idea that education has become both mechanized and bureaucratized, narrowed down through succeeding generations of reform, lies at the heart of the 'free school' movement. It is this idea that poses both the paradox and the push to seek new alternatives for education. It has also lead the movement to reject some of the most cherished beliefs that surround the education system.

The creed of the 'free school' movement has four articles of faith. Upon them rests the ideology of the movement and much of the critique levelled by its acolytes against the education system in general. Translated into practical terms, they go far in explaining many of the differences between the 'official school' and the 'free school'. They are: freedom of access; freedom to learn in one's own time; freedom to use resources available in the community for educational purposes; and freedom to organize schools other than those provided by local education authorities. If we take these four freedoms each in turn, examining them in the light of what happens in the 'official' school by contrast with what is hoped will take place in the 'free school', we can, little by little, build up a picture of the 'free school' movement.

Freedom of Access

Though the creation of an industrialized society, the school represents in many respects a medieval throwback vis à vis the community in which it is set. Like the keep of a local brigand chieftain, it keeps little contact with its serfs. The drawbridge, let down at 8.30 a.m., and again at 4 p.m., effectively keeps the community at bay. Links between school and its neighbourhood are channelled into formal occasions: prize day, parent teachers' association (where it exists) or careers conventions. As with the medieval fortress, interlopers are admitted only after swearing fealty, agreeing to abide by the rules set by the professional barons of education. Increasingly the role of the family in educating or bringing up its children passes into the hands of professionals whose responsibility is to local education administrators rather than to parents. In the context of the 'official school' this development has two results. Firstly, it is progressively detached from the community, unresponsive to, and with very little understanding of the very specific educational and cultural needs of that community. Secondly, the school assumes a paternalism all the greater for there being little legal possibilities of countering it.

By throwing the school open to a co-operative partnership between parents, children and teachers, the 'free school' movement aims firstly at involving parents more actively in the education of their children, reversing, hopefully, the tendency to cut down the role of the family in this respect. In short, the 'free school' seeks to restore a balance between the informal upbringing that has by tradition fallen to the family and the formal instruction that takes place in school. Pushed to its limits, the purpose of opening up the school in this way is to remove, as far as possible, the distinction between education on the one hand and instruction on the other. Secondly, the 'free school' movement hopes, by binding the school with the community, to return the school to a position at the centre of the community in which instruction of children is but part of its wide ranging activities. This latter intention is particularly interesting since it forms what one might call the mythology of the education system as it is seen by the 'free schoolers'. It implies some previous state of grace when the school was the centre of the community, from which position it has departed, abrogating the responsibilities that befell to it in times past. Certainly, it is possible to believe that Goldsmith's village school master, a paradigm of rustic erudition and poverty, played a certain role in the community. But mass education as it evolved over the past 100 years has never been in this position. Be this as it may, the idea of restoring usurped or forgotten links between school and community is, for all its historic inaccuracy, a powerful driving force in the movement.

Freedom to Learn in one's Own Time

Over the past few years, one of the most interesting developments in education has been the breakdown in lockstep learning. The introduction of project work, of self directed enquiry has shifted the emphasis in learning from the uniform achievement of classes grouped by ability towards individual acquisition of knowledge and skills, each child proceeding at a pace suitable to him or her. Such developments recognize firstly that children do not learn at the same rate, and secondly, that intellectual development and maturity alter from individual to individual. These changes are part of a fundamental shift in the philosophy of education in which external constraint and sanctions are replaced by motivation and the will generated by the individual to learn. In the 'official school', this shift in attitude has lead to the individualization of the timetable with its attendant possibilities of creating a curriculum for each particular pupil in the light of his needs and requirements. Agreed, the number of schools that have taken up individual tailor made curricula are as yet small. Theirs is the work of the pioneers in the state education system. By contrast, 'free schools' make this pioneering stance part of the basic feature of the school. Attendance is not compulsory, school hours are not fixed. Their curriculum, such as it is, depends entirely on self-directed learning. Such a free-wheeling situation has important repercussions both on the role of the teacher and upon the school. By placing the control over the curriculum in the hands of the pupil, the 'free school' teacher is reduced to being a voluntary co-ordinator of interests.

In 'official schools' there is a hierarchy of prestige and status closely linked to the type of subject. Professional standing is often judged by whether one teaches a subject that leads to higher education. Thus the notion of a compulsory curriculum is fundamental where it is not the *raison d'être*, to the status of members within the teaching profession. By removing the compulsory nature of a standardized curriculum, the 'free school' offers a serious challenge in two areas. Firstly, it removes the hierarchy within the teaching staff. Secondly, it removes the exclusivism of education from the teaching profession. In theory, though it still remains largely untried, 'de-professionalizing' the school is regarded by 'free schoolers' as an important element in opening up the school to the community.

Furthermore, children's interests are not likely to fit in with the official notion of education being academic, vocational or technical. Indeed, the 'free schoolers' have argued, the whole purpose of education is hampered by the artificial division into subjects of greater or lesser repute, a division which has little foundation other than in the minds of teachers. If the school is to tackle the full educational needs of children, it must open itself up to as wide ranging a series of skills and abilities for educating as possible. And these do not necessarily reside in the education profession. Parents with special interests and skills should, they point out, be allowed to take part in the teaching.

Freedom to Use the Resources in the Community

Just as the community is encouraged to enter the school, and as we have seen, to take part in teaching, so the school should extend itself to the community. That the school should go on the streets, is a neat reversal of the belief that its one purpose was to keep children off them! The idea, however, is not the exclusive property of the 'free schoolers'. Already, in many areas of this country, in particular the planning of schools in the new town of Milton Keynes, it groups schools together with the major community centres and with such services as libraries, adult education centres and clinics. Both architecturally as well as administratively, the concentration of community services in one area goes part way to making the school the centre of town life. The 'free schoolers' take the development further. By using the streets as a classroom, by encouraging firms, offices and industries to provide practical experience of working in them, the community itself can become an educational resource. Few schools in Britain have as yet tried this experiment, partly because they lack the resources, partly because 'free schools' still remain on the educational fringe in this country. Even so, experiments on these lines have been carried out in Philadelphia, though not without opposition. The argument behind such proposals does make sense in many regards. However well equipped, no school can hope to command the resources, training and information that is to be found in an industrial society. Still less does it have the wherewithal to reproduce them in miniature.

Freedom to Organize Schools other than Those Set Up by Local Education Authorities

Since the abolition of the local School Boards in 1902, control over education has rested in the hands of local councils working through the local education administration. Indeed, education was one of the earliest areas of government at local level to feel the effects of rapid bureaucratization. Community control over its schools is at best indirect: at worst, non-existent. The school is as isolated administratively as it is educationally from its local setting. Of course, there have always been ways in which schools could be set up, controlled by parents or their appointees. But they were – and still are – limited to the private fee-paying sector. If upper and middle class parents enjoyed some element of control over their schools, or at least the financial possibility of setting up their own school, working class parents have had to make do with an education provided for them, rather than by them. The freedom to set up schools outside the state sector of education is an important plank in the ideology of the 'free school' movement and one that links them with certain developments which took place towards the end of the last century. We will discuss this point in greater detail later. Suffice it to point out at this stage that many of the arguments put forward in support of a non-fee-paying autonomous sector in the education system are very similar to those used by supporters of the public schools. The right of parents – and for that matter of children as well – to choose between state and 'free schools' is the exact mirror image to the argument tediously exhumed whenever a Secretary of State wishes to defend the top twenty-five schools. Curiously, even the supporters of the 'free school' have never presented them as possible alternatives to the public school: only to state schools.

Support for the 'Free School'

That the 'free school' movement is dedicated to reforming
state schools whilst ostensibly ignoring public schools is,
not without reason, seen as one of its major weaknesses.
Educational apartheid remains apartheid, regardless of
whether supported by parental ambition, money, status
consciousness or by the heart-felt desire to liberate the
schools from the shackles of educational administrators or
to restore it to the community in general. Why, then, are
'free schoolers' so opposed to state education? There are
many different strands that go to make up the 'free school'
movement – an ideological Joseph's Coat of many Colours – but one thing they share in common is the belief
that radical reform of state education from within is
impossible. Reform can only be brought about in state
education by creating an alternative system. This dilemma
is one common to many radical reforms at their outset, be
they political or for a particular issue. It is the old question
that faced the Labour movement ninety years ago and
which it eventually resolved by setting itself up as a political force working from within Parliament. But the fact
that this debate still colours the 'free school' movement tells
us much about its state of political development, though
less about the practicality of its programme.

To some extent, however, there is justification for their
views. State education has proved remarkably impervious
to the more radical aspects of educational innovation.
Though the past few years have seen a thaw in this direction, progressive education has remained largely confined
to the private sector. In part, this is due to the separation
of reform movements in education into two clear strands.
The first has been concerned with extending to the majority the benefits and opportunities enjoyed by the few. This
group, we might call it the official reform movement, is

usually backed by the National Union of Teachers and the Trades Union movement. The second, however, concerned itself more with the content of education, with reforming the ethos, the curriculum and the internal relationships of the school with its inmates. The latter detached itself clearly from the issues of educational opportunity around the turn of the century, taking refuge in the private sector (for example, Abbotsholme, and later Gordonstoun, Summerhill and Bryanston). Whilst the former movement sought to extend traditional patterns of education to the mass of children, the latter sought to innovate within the narrow confines of the elite. Against this background, it is apparent that the 'free school' movement falls between two stools. On the one hand, it is opposed to the reform that created official schools, whilst on the other seeks to conjure up a movement destined to reform the education of large numbers of children using the same type of reform associated with elitist education.

It is perhaps this very ambivalence towards the question of educational reform that can account for the growing popularity of the 'free school' movement. The 'free school' can be upheld by widely different groups with widely differing motives. The argument in favour of a 'free' sector in state education comes in very handy when the 'free' sector of private education is fighting for its life. The changeover to comprehensive education means the grammar school can no longer be used as an outer bastion of defence for the public schools. Some other feat of mental gymnastics is required to justify the privilege of the purse. On the other hand, there is considerable evidence from social surveys and other sociological studies to suggest that the school has little effect on alleviating the problems of educational and social deprivation. In many cases, it appears to compound them, conferring advantage where advantage exists. But the powerlessness of the

schools to compensate for deprivation is largely inevitable, given that the causes of it lie far outside the school
system. To believe otherwise is to believe that education,
on its own, can alter a situation that results from economic
factors, whereas the school – even the 'free school' – has to
operate within the bounds of a capitalist economic system
that conditions deprivation. To believe, as do many
supporters of 'free schools', that institutional change, the
de-professionalization of education and the expansion of
the school into the community is an automatic alleviation
of problems facing education today is to carry conviction to
the uncritical heights of religious fervour. The millennium,
brothers, will not start with the White Lion Free School!

Yet, the growing popularity of 'free school' theory is
undisputed. Nor can it be attributed entirely to the sinister
machinations of the defenders of public schools. Still less
can its popularity rest totally on the power of ideological
conviction, however strongly held. Perhaps the most
powerful influence and one that, in the long run, could turn
out decisive, has been the raising of the school leaving age.
As many teachers and administrators have pointed out, it
places additional strain on the school to provide for those
remaining the extra year. It creates greater problems of
discipline amongst pupils who are forced to stay where
previously they would have left school. 'Free schools'
could well provide a useful solution – at least on a short-
term basis – to an otherwise potentially explosive situation,
by absorbing the dissident and leaving the school to concentrate on its more tractable pupils. In short, the 'free
schools' could well provide a palliative by which official
schools could ignore the real educational problems merely
highlighted by the new fifth year. How far such a consideration will prompt local education authorities to support the 'free schools' in the future remains at the moment
a matter of speculation.

The Ideology of the 'Free Schools'

But if support for the 'free schools' comes from widely different sources, so also does its ideology. The theory of the 'free school' has three main strands. The first – and perhaps the most routine therefore the least interesting – is an extension of community politics into the school. This strand does not necessarily challenge the content or the type of education the school purveys. Rather the school is ancillary to a wider political movement, often identified with the Liberal and Labour parties or those sections of them concerned with the devolution of power. For them, the school is an example through which devolution and community politics can be played out.

The second strand in the ideological composition of the movement is connected with the student generation whose political involvement in educational reform dated from the time of the troubles in higher education during the late 1960s. For this group, which can be identified with the New Left, though not exclusively so, the move into the 'free school' question extends the battle for reform that began with the universities.

The third strand in the reform is one of the most interesting developments in present day education: the re-emergence of Libertarian involvement in educational change and the growing acceptance of an educational equivalent of workers' control. To a very high degree, the theory and justification of 'free schools' derives from the writings of Libertarian educationists such as Paul Goodman, Jules Henry and Everett Reimer.

In the main, however, the theory of 'free schooling' evolved from work carried out into the education systems of the third world, principally in the writings of Ivan Illich, a Roman Catholic priest and educationalist working in Mexico. Illich cannot, primarily, be identified with the 'free school' movement so much as with the other popular cult of the moment, 'de-schooling'. The difference between the 'free schooler' and the 'de-schooler' is that whilst the former tries to extend the purpose of the school, the latter questions the need to continue with school at all. One of the most unusual features of the 'free school' movement is its use of models derived from the education systems of underdeveloped countries. There are many reasons why the third world has such fascination. In the first place, it brings together the otherwise disparate elements of the New Left and the Libertarians. In the second place, the creation of mass education systems in those countries has been concentrated into a far shorter period of time than in the West. Consequently, the problems faced by third world education systems are far more acute and therefore far more visible and immediate than those countries whose education has developed over a longer span of time. In the third place, the underdeveloped countries are passing through a process of social change which in Europe took place gradually over the past century. The motives for creating education systems in the third world, systems that are all too often pale replicas of those found in the West, provide an interesting explanation – with a dash of historical hindsight – for those that lay behind the establishment of education systems in industrialized countries. In short, the third world, and principally Latin America, provides a fruitful analogy with a situation that many supporters of the 'free school' feel exists in industrial countries and one that permits considerable insight.

The key concept, the link point between the third world and the 'free school' movement, lies in the notion of cultural imperialism. Most of the education systems in third world countries are, as we have pointed out, exports of the West, some the shards and legacies of colonial times, some created later as a means to consolidate economic imperialism by furnishing a docile, yet suitably trained, labour force. Just as the American model of the school has been exported to Latin America in the baggage trains of US Aid Programmes, so too, from the point of view of the radical sociologist is the school system in Britain an example of cultural imperialism. The school is, effectively, a middle class instrument of cultural colonialization amongst the working class. Like the mission schools in underdeveloped countries, assimilating selected members of the indigenous population to support the economic and social nexus of colonial exploitation, so the school assimilates selected members of the working class into the ranks of the middle class. Alternatively to its role as a means of social mobility, it assigns each according to his lot to various levels in the labour force. By contrast, the 'free school's' aim is to detach education from the economic system which at present it underpins. The school should not automatically act as an instrument for transmitting middle class culture. Lastly, though agreement on this point differs, the 'free school' aims at creating a political consciousness amongst its students which, hopefully, will turn the school from consolidating the education and social status quo into an active agent for social and political change.

Other 'Free School' Systems: an Historical Excursion

Aims such as these are not, however, novel. Many of them formed the bedrock of the Socialist Sunday schools that flourished in Britain in the period between 1890 and 1930. Where they differ from the 'free schools' is in respect firstly of their political involvement and secondly of their relationship with the state education system. Whereas Socialist Sunday schools sought to throw up a future generation of political leaders for the working class and Trades

Union movements, the 'free schools' are not as yet identified with an official political party. And whilst the Socialist Sunday schools existed alongside the state education system to which their pupils went during weekdays, the 'free school' seeks to provide an alternative system. It is perhaps not coincidence that the nearest equivalent to the present day 'free school' movement is to be found in the French Trades Union movement towards the end of the last century. The coincidence is that both of them share a Libertarian ideology. Unlike the British Trades Unions, the French were not dedicated to the notion of working through Parliament. On the contrary, they acted as the vanguard for a future working class revolution, a revolution that would be carried out through the use of the General Strike as a political instrument. The aim of the French Trades Union movement was therefore to educate its members into understanding the crucial role of the General Strike as a means by which capitalism would be swept away. It was not socialist. Indeed, it regarded socialists as political opportunists, parliamentary chameleons, and an unsavoury species inhabiting a jungle with which they would have no truck.

The heart of the French Trades Unions, or Syndicates, lay in the *Bourses de Travail* (Workers' Labour Exchanges) which provided information on jobs, organized strike committees as well as having a flourishing education section. Organized by Fernand Pelloutier, the Secretary General of the Labour Exchanges, the schools inside the French Trades Union movement bear a remarkable resemblance to the present day 'free schools', a similarity both of ideology and of purpose. The schools did not survive Pelloutier's death in 1899, but they were, within the context of an anarcho-syndicalist Labour movement, a remarkable attempt to create an alternative system. Generally, the task of the Labour Exchanges within which the schools operated went far beyond the mundane matters of trades union organization. They were intended to provide the nucleus of a future society based on syndacalist theory. They were, in Pelloutier's words, 'the seedbeds of the future', replicas in miniature of a society which would shake itself out on the morning after the revolution. In modern parlance, they were the alternative society – a commune derived not from the ill digested dreams of nut cutlet eaters, but from the Paris Commune of 1871. The schools inside the Labour Exchanges were founded with the specific idea of providing an *alternative*, a system based on totally different ideological premisses, to the state education system whose creation was comparatively recent (1883). Pelloutier's 'free schools' attempted to combat state ideology even before it had become established. They were also designed to prevent the assimilation of able working class children into the ranks of the middle class. For, as Pelloutier remarked, the working class movement could only become an autonomous agency for social change if it did not allow itself to become decapitated of leadership. Well before the phenomenon was identified by bourgeois sociologists and anthropologists, Pelloutier recognized the importance of publicly provided education as a means both of social mobility and the political socialization that follows from it. More important still, he recognized the consequences for radical social change.

The parallels between the embryonic system of education Pelloutier tried to kindle in the French Trades Union movement and the 'free schools' today are not chance coincidence. Both 'free schools' and Labour Exchanges seek to create an autonomous sector of education outside the official state sector. Both seek to create a focus of community interests, the 'free schools' for the community as a rather general and diffuse idea, the French Labour Exchanges, specifically for the working class. Both

Labour Exchanges and 'free schools' aim at finding a counterbalance to the growing power of middle class enculturation and the extension of middle class values, norms, aspirations and attitudes to working class parents and children by way of the school. Both attempt to forge what one can only describe as an integrated community, the first around a political idea and a political movement, the second around a particular neighbourhood.

'Free Schools': a Phenomenon of Transition

The revival of Libertarian theories of education and the fact that these ideas are re-emerging into the light of day after an interval of some seventy or eighty years is important. Why, though, should they suddenly have gained such attraction after having lain fallow for so long?

A particularly plausible explanation for the reappearance of the fight between Libertarian and institutionalized education is to be found in the social, economic and political circumstances in which it grew up. Much of the study of Libertarian movements, and those in France in particular, has emphasized the role of wide ranging social change during the periods when Libertarianism was accepted. In the case of the French Trades Union movement, it was the transition of society from an *agrarian* to an *industrial* basis. Anarcho-syndicalism and its Libertarian overtones is therefore linked with periods of flux when the old order is breaking down, but before a new pattern has firmly emerged. In effect, the 'free school' movement can be made to conform very realistically to this analysis. It coincides with the transition of society from an *industrial* basis in which education is geared to future job requirements, social control and political formation to a *post industrial* society in which education can no longer be geared to the notion of a single occupation throughout one lifetime, and in which the school can no longer be said to be the major agency for social control.

Indeed, many of the tensions that exist in present day education systems stem from the fact that whilst in some respects society has made the transition from industrial to post industrial modes of production, the school system, based on the requirements of a previous era, has not. Indeed, many of the problems that fire current controversy in education – for instance, the consequences of affluence, relative deprivation, education for leisure, compensatory education – not only reflect the inadequacies of the school system to meet the problems thrown up by social change, but its inadequacy in remedying problems that have been recognized even in the earliest stages of industrialization. The school is equipped to deal with yesterday's problems tomorrow, but never today's now.

In general, the 'free school' movement and the theories from which it derives much of its influence – a theory contained in the writings of Paul Goodman and Ivan Illich – largely reflect these shortcomings. At eighty years remove, Pelloutier faced similar problems. Firstly, the problem of the transition from an agrarian community to an industrial community. Secondly, the problem of creating autonomous institutions capable of resisting the official state ideology. As we have seen, the solutions to the problems of transition from an agrarian to an industrial society in the case of the schools inside the Labour Exchanges and secondly, in the case of the transition from an industrial to a post industrial society in the case of the 'free schools' are basically very similar. The first aimed at a republic of communes in which the school was part. The second aims at a republic of local schools of which the community is part. The degree of similarity between the two movements suggests that the appearance and acceptance of Libertarian ideas in education is linked with periods of political and social fluidity:

or, put another way, those periods of transition and change in the mode of production during which patterns of education are inadequate but during which also, an adequate solution in terms of institutional change has yet to be reached.

If this is so, then the 'free school' movement is not so much an agency of social change as an example of changes in society imposing on education from without. Assuming this is so for the moment, then it would appear that the 'free school' movement is a transitional, if not a transitory phenomenon, useful as a critique of the education system as it is at present, but without the power to provide either long-term solutions or the institutional framework for their enactment. To the Marxist educationalists, it is an interesting example of the dialectic in which the present school system forms the thesis, the 'free school' movement the antithesis from which might spring a fruitful, though future, synthesis for an education system in the second half of the twentieth century. That the 'free school' acts as a species of midwife to educational change explains much of its recent popularity in educational circles. It provides a nice and somewhat cosy debating point for retired radicals in Teacher Training Colleges as they quaff their half pints with the chaps.

Three Groups of 'Free School' Supporters

Though we have already looked at some of the main sources of support for the 'free school' movement it is nevertheless worthwhile to take a closer glimpse at the motives of some of those most prominently engaged in it. Opposition to state education is, we suggested, one of the threads running through the movement. Combined in this theme are three different ideological currents. The first has its being in the nineteenth-century classical Liberal doctrine of non-intervention by the state in matters which are felt to be the concern of the individual: laissez-faire in the education world. The second springs from the traditional hostility of the Libertarian movement towards any extension of the state. It differs from the Liberal doctrine in that it is opposed to the state under any guise whatsoever, be it the capitalist state, the socialist, regardless of whether its policies are laissez-faire or interventionist. The third opposes state intervention because, in the words of Everett Reimer, 'Schools serve societies which dedicate themselves to consumption . . . they assume that man wants principally to consume and that in order to consume he must bind himself to the wheel of endless production.' This latter, essentially the view of the Crypto Marxist element supporting 'free schools', regards state schools as the instrument which creates the necessary values of obedience, submission, industriousness and discipline that ultimately, in an industrial society, mould the psychological framework upholding the relationship of different classes to the means of production. Translated into a post industrial society, the school performs the same role, inculcating the necessary social values to uphold a consumer society. From a truly Marxist viewpoint, however, this analysis is defective. It emphasizes consumption as an evil in itself, an objection that seems more akin to the condemnation of ostentation and to the sumptary laws of sixteenth-century England – a religious rather than a material criticism.

Of these three strands in the ideology of the 'free school', the Liberal is ambivalent on two counts. Firstly because what was held up to be the doctrine of rugged individualism – of non-intervention by the state in matters of education – can be the reverse side of public indifference to the question of educational reform. In the past it has lead to private affluence and public squalor. There is nothing to suggest it will not do so in the future. Secondly, because it preserves, nominally under the cloak of variety of choice between different types of education, a division of the education system into groups that closely correspond to the social classes. The Liberal argument that the powers of the state should be curbed lest education breed a soulless conformity – the vision of 1984 with the policy of 1884 – begs the question 'Who will have the choice anyway?' That 80 per cent of parents have not been able to choose the type of education they would wish for their children has not, even under the education system existing for the past thirty years, brought about any greater conformity in the behaviour of either young people or their parents.

Both Libertarian and the Crypto Marxist opposition to the power of the state and their backing of autonomous schools outside its purlieu derives from slightly different premisses. The first of these is the growing concern with the increasing integration of education and industry, a process particularly pronounced over the past few years. This is not to say that links between school and factory have not existed before. They have. But in recent years the role of industry under several guises has become more powerful. One of these areas has been curriculum reform. Much of the innovation in this area has been designed to bring the school system more in line with the demands of scientific and technological manpower. The role of the Nuffield Foundation has been especially important, redirecting the education system towards producing scientifically trained students for the middle and upper management levels. There can be no doubt that the basis of educational reform has come increasingly to rely on technocratic considerations all over the West. Education is construed in terms of national manpower needs and the needs of the individual are accommodated so long as they fit in with this predetermined framework.

The second premiss that inspired to varying degrees

Libertarians and Crypto Marxists to support the 'free school' is an extension of issues raised by student movements of the mid and late 1960s. Many of the reforms demanded by the student movement proved either abortive or short-lived because of failure to gain support from other sections of the community. Compared with the problems of inner city children and the conditions of vast numbers of children in ill-equipped secondary and primary schools, the student revolt was very much the hagglings of a gilded youth, the whimper of the well-off. It is, of course, difficult to determine how far that student generation has changed its tactics. But it is probable that many of them realized fundamental reform in education would be more fruitful if begun at the bottom rather than by spectacular confrontations at the top. Certainly a strong contingent of student radicals has moved into the 'free schools'. To some, the 'free schools' continue the popular tactic of the student revolt, creating red bases as a counter ideology to the hierarchy of authority found in 'official schools'.

Alongside those who see the 'free schools' as red bases – the educational equivalent of the urban guerilla – runs another strand: that of setting up schools to preserve working class culture. Though not shared by all supporters of the movement, it is nevertheless regarded as a task of prime importance by those working in the Scotland Road Free School in Liverpool, for instance. On the face of things there is much to be said for this approach. Official schools act largely as an agency purveying the goodies of middle class culture, forming the right attitudes, or at least those seen as desirable by teachers – industriousness, punctuality, competitive achievement and the desire to get on. The result, as many studies have shown, is to require a working class child to live in two worlds, two cultural environments – home and school, whereas middle class children live in a single cultural milieu with the school acting as an extension to the home, reinforcing its attitudes. By creating a school based on the culture of the locality, rather than divorced from it, the 'free schoolers' hope to provide an additional dimension to the equality of educational opportunity that cannot be realized by 'official schools'.

The 'Free School': Some Implications

Having discussed some of the motives behind the 'free school' movement, we are now faced with the final and perhaps crucial question: what, if any, are the broad implications? For example, how would the education system be affected by a further upsurge of 'free schools'? The first of these implications falls in the area of reform itself. We have seen that 'free schoolers', some explicitly others more tacitly, take the view that reform of state education is impossible, where not irrelevant. Reform is, however, possible but only in those areas where the power of the state apparatus, if not diminished, is at least less effective or – depending on one's viewpoint – negligent. Such a belief runs deeply in the idea that autonomous schools should be set up outside the state system. In other words, educational reform can only take place in those marginal areas, inner city twilight zones and places of massive deprivation.

It is difficult, however, to see how 'free schools' as they are at present constituted could have much impact upon downtown areas without the financial backing of official bodies. It is one thing to run a small school, staffed by volunteers, run on a shoe string, it is another to create schools capable of dealing with large numbers of children. Though the use of volunteers does smack of a return to teaching as a vocation, an attitude which, exploited by generations of administrators, has been one of the root causes for the present ill-paid position of the teaching profession. Many 'free schools' depend on hand outs supplementing their funds by jumble sales and the occasional gift from well wishers. In some areas, Liverpool is one, some backing comes from the local authority which sees the 'free school' as a useful instrument for coping with the drop out problem. This support raises several issues, all of which are important for the future development of the movement. The first is to what extent can a school be said to be 'free' if it is in the end dependent on local authorities? Local authorities apart, all schools are in any case subject to the requirements and regulations of the Department of Education and Science. Since subjection of this sort means ultimately control, to what extent is it possible to maintain the fiction of being an autonomous 'free school' outside the state sector? The fact is that as soon as the 'free school' movement depends on state approval it is part of the state system.

Some 'free schoolers' will, rightly, point out that possible bureaucratic hostility is the least important of the problems the 'free school' has to tackle. Agreed, but the implications of local authority support go far beyond the merely quibbling over the number of lavatories. We must also examine the motives of such bodies for supporting the movement. The main one, we would suggest, is to defuse the drop out problem, alternatively to reduce truanting. Such motives have wide ranging implications for the education system in general, not just the 'free school'. The 'free schools' are being asked to take over the child minding aspect of education, keeping young people off the streets and, to some extent, off the labour market. From this we can suggest that one of the reasons for supporting 'free schools' stems directly from the parlous economic position in which the country nearly always finds itself when it comes to expenditure in public undertakings.

There is thus an apparent contradiction between the purpose of the 'free school' seen by its supporters and the purpose to which it will be put by local education authorities.

By catering for children who drop out, the 'free school' is engaged in recreating an education system very similar to the bipartite model, though on different grounds. A rapid examination of the bipartite education system shows us that the division between grammar schools on the one hand, for children of academic ability, was matched by the secondary modern school intended to take the remainder. From the standpoint of the educational sociologist, the difference between the schools does not stop merely at the difference in education each provided. The grammar school catered as well for children destined for social mobility in varying degrees. The secondary modern coped with the majority who were not. Similarly, the 'free schools', catering for drop outs, are also catering for the socially immobile. Where they exist alongside official schools they represent to some extent the survival of the universally condemned two class education system. Furthermore, they help to keep alive the idea of education being mainly about social mobility by removing from schools those who are not socially mobile. The result can only be further to elevate in official schools the notion of manpower planning and the further reduction of education to a process of mechanistic training, rather than a means of acquiring self development.

Many of the elements currently emerging as the crisis in the classroom are not solved by returning to bipartite education. Indeed, truanting and the growing dissatisfaction of children with school are themselves products of a divided education system. To pose a solution in terms of reverting to the cause of the problem is, at best a logical fallacy, at worst chuckleheaded. The problems faced by comprehensive schools – often inflated beyond all proportion by reactionary opponents of change – are made worse by continuing teaching methods and teacher attitudes which, though suitable in a divided education system, are not in a unified one. We have yet to see a truly comprehensive curriculum and learning situation in widespread use. In the meantime, we should avoid thinking in terms of a problem sector in secondary education. Problems are not solved by wishing them away, nor is the problem student any less a problem by being consigned to elegant oblivion in some amateur institution for the intractable.

These are not the only objections to the expansion of 'free schools'. One of the most powerful arguments against dividing education according to types of student – be it by ability or by behaviour – is that it removes much of the pressure for reform, dissipating rather than concentrating it. In effect, and we have seen it at work these fifteen or twenty years past, a divided education system limits the area of reform to particular sectors leaving unchallenged many of the fundamental issues posed by the continuation of an education system that still remains profoundly elitist in operation.

'Free schools', then, are fundamentally subversive of a comprehensive education system. Far more than that, however, they represent the disturbing spectacle not merely of pupils who have freaked out of education but in many cases of teachers as well. It could well be that support for the movement is but a tactical withdrawal from current controversy in education the better to return later. For all that, the retreat to small, marginal enclaves in the education system appears suspiciously like a rush to avoid the more immediate and pressing questions that demand reform.

The flight into Camden Town, to Islington or to Scotland Road, Liverpool, presents no enduring challenge to the question of who controls the education system for the majority. It does not solve the problem presented to state education by the public schools. Even less does it recognize the problem of influence and control exercised by particular institutions over education, for instance, the hold of Balliol College, Oxford, over the Department of Education and Science which has continued since the 1920s and 1930s. The paradox of the 'free school' movement is that, preoccupied with the reforms that *might* be necessary for the day after tomorrow, it is less interested in those taking place today.

This not to say that many features of 'free schooling' should be discarded. There are many that can and should be adapted to the state school. Freedom of access and freedom to learn in one's own time are perhaps the most exciting, though many of these have already been adopted in some comprehensive schools. But unless 'free schoolers' are prepared to battle for their introduction into state education, then theirs is a movement that cannot be regarded with any seriousness. If it remains on the fringes of state education, opposed to its extension to all children in a single type of school, or unprepared to face up to the major issues on current reform, the 'free school' must be seen as the *break-up* of radicalism in education, not the *breakthrough*.

Reading Guide

On 'free schools'
  W. Kenneth Richmond, *The Free School*, Methuen, £2·90
  Ivan Illich, *De Schooling Society*, Penguin: Education Special
  Everette Reimar, *School is Dead*, Penguin: Education Special

On the French labour movement
  R. R. Ridley, *Anarcho Syndicalism in France*, CUP, £5
Unfortunately most of the books on this aspect of the article are

extremely difficult to get, few exist outside national libraries.
None of them are available in English. However, for readers
who have time, enormous patience and outrageous persistence
there is an article by Allan Spitzer on Pelloutier's educational
ideas and social policy in the *International Journal of Social
History*, 1963.

If you would like a complete list of **Arrow books**
please send a postcard to
P.O. Box 29, Douglas, Isle of Man, Great Britain.

On the following pages are details of some other titles available in Arrow

THE UNION MAKES US STRONG

The British Working Class Its Politics and Trade Unionism

by Tony Lane

Central to an understanding of the political condition of the working class is its one durable monument: the trades unions. Traditionally the working man has looked to his union, – and its political arm, the Labour Party, – for the power to bring radical change. But this book argues that the origins and structure of these organisations can only act for the accommodation of labour with capital.

By considering the history of the labour movement Tony Lane looks at the political consciousness of the rank and file, and the ways in which union leaders at all levels tend to become isolated from the man on the shop floor. In particular he explodes the cherished myth that the failures of socialism can be laid at the doors of a succession of leaders who have 'betrayed' the movement. His conclusion is that the power to force much needed social change must be spear-headed by a socialist party.

MEET YOUR FRIENDLY SOCIAL SYSTEM
by Peter Laurie

In moments of despondency we say, 'Well that's the system. You can't beat the system'. But what is the 'system'? How does it work? And how does it manipulate us?

Peter Laurie's new book looks at the ways the system controls us. His examination reveals not a conspiracy of cunning men but an inescapable social structure in which each of us is locked rigidly into his place. He argues that nearly every feature of our lives – poverty, good taste, shiny shoes, sex, social workers, crime, dope, pension funds – contributes to this iron pattern; and that before we can change it, we must understand it.

This is a very unsettling book, but one that will strike a chord in anyone who suspects that the world has gone awry. Before the world can get better it will have to get worse. But how much worse? Certainly after reading this book it will never look the same again.

CITIZENS RIGHTS SERIES

General Editor: Frank Field, Director of the Child Poverty Action Group

The legislation of the Welfare State aimed to give ordinary people a much better deal. But politicians and lawyers overlooked one crucial fact. We don't all speak or understand their language.

Unlike the official handouts this series is written by experts whose work is to help people understand and claim their rights. In other words it has been written with you in mind. Each guide can be read without referring to any other material. They can deal with all the main issues where you, the citizen, find that 'they' are not telling you all you ought to know.

First two titles in this series are:
SUPPLEMENTARY BENEFIT RIGHTS by Ruth Lister
LEGAL RIGHTS by Henry Hodge

Education or Domination?